외국어는 경쟁력!

외국어는 당신을 남들보다 우월하게 만들어주는 경쟁력입니다. 외국어는 당신이 앞으로 하게 될 일, 명함에 새겨질 직함, 받게 될 급여 수준, 타게 될 자동차의 배기량, 살게 될 지역과 집의 크기, 사귀게 될 사람들의 부류, 배우자의 외모, 자녀들이 다닐 학교, 즐겨 입는 옷의 브랜드, 여름마다 가기 될 휴양지, 그리고 그 밖의 많은 것을 결정하는 데 중요한 역할을 한다는 것을 기억하십시오. 언어는 힘입니다.

PASSIONATE ABOUT YOUR SUCCESS!!
당신의 성공에 열광하겠습니다.

Cow & Bridge Publishing Co.
도서출판 소와다리

WELCOME TO NEW YORK GRAMMAR SCHOOL!

COW & BRIDGE
PUBLISHING COMPANY

Web site : www.cafe.naver.com/sowadari
3ga-302, 6-21, 40th St., Guwolro, Namgu, Incheon, #402-848 South Korea
Telephone 0505-719-7787 Facsimile 0505-719-7788 Email sowadari@naver.com

NEW YORK GRAMMAR SCHOOL 1
by Grant Taylor

웰컴투 뉴욕그래머스쿨1 2012 © Cow & Bridge Publishing Co. all rights reserved.
이 책의 저작권 및 출판권에 관련된 모든 제반 권리는 도서출판 소와다리가 소유합니다.

No part of this publication may be repoduced,
stored in retrieval system or transmitted in any form or by any means
without the prior written permission of the bona fide copyright holder.

이 책은 지적재산권법 및 저작권법에 의거하여 보호를 받는 저작물이므로 저작권 및 출판권 소유자의 서면 동의 없이는
책의 일부, 혹은 전부를 무단으로 복제하여 배포하거나 전자적인 방식으로 변환하여 전송할 수 없습니다.

ISBN 978-89-98046-03-3 14740
Printed in Korea

웰컴투 뉴욕그래머스쿨 1
NEW YORK GRAMMAR SCHOOL
ELEMENTARY & INTERMEDIATE COURSE

ELEMENTARY & INTERMEDIATE COURSE
(PUT YOUR NAME ON YOUR CERTIFICATE)

Certificate For Admission

CERTIFICATE FOR ADMISSION
TO
NEW YORK GRAMMAR SCHOOL
AMERICAN ENGLISH GRAMMAR ELEMENTARY & INTERMEDIATE COURSES

This is to certify that _____your name here_____

has completed the Preliminary Course for mastering Amern English in _____your school here_____

and is qualified to enrol in the American English Grammar Elementary & Intermediate Courses

in the New York Grammar School.

Given at your place, this ___date___ th day of ___month___ in the year of ___year___ .

_____
Head Teacher

_____   _____
Publisher   Asst. Teacher

WELCOME TO NEW YORK GRAMMAR SCHOOL!
뉴욕 그래머스쿨에 입학하신 것을 축하합니다!

뉴욕 그래머스쿨은 영어를 모국어로 사용하지 않는 세계 각국의 학생들이 모여 있는 가상의 랭기지스쿨입니다. 학생들 대부분은 단시간 내에 영어를 배우기 위해 뉴욕 그래머스쿨로 어학연수를 왔으며, 중고등학교 수준의 기초적인 영어 문법을 습득한 상태입니다. 따라서 본 스쿨의 수업은 일체의 군더더기를 배제한 고등학교 수준의 기초 문법만으로 일상생활에서의 간결한 의사소통은 물론 비즈니스 상황에서 쓰기에 손색이 없는 품격 있는 미국 영어를 구사하는 것을 목적으로 합니다.

또한 **뉴욕 그래머스쿨**에서는 수업방식 안내 이후, 영어를 제외한 기타 언어로 된 어떤 문법 설명도 제공하지 않습니다. 그러나 설명이 필요 없을 정도로 직관적인 예문과 선생님의 질문에 간단명료한 영어로 답하는 수업을 통해 학생들은 스스로 문법을 익히고 자유로운 커뮤니케이션 능력을 기를 수 있습니다. 이번 입학생과 본 스쿨의 선생님 중 한국인은 당신 혼자뿐이기 때문에 다른 한국인 친구나 한국 선생님의 도움은 전혀 받을 수 없습니다. 다만 수업 중 한국어로 된 다른 참고자료를 이용하여 문제를 푸는 것은 제한하지 않습니다.

그럼, 당신에게 신의 가호가 있기를.
God bless you!

Head Teacher, Grant Taylor

TO THE STUDENT

뉴욕 그래머스쿨의 레슨은 ①문법학습 ②듣고 말하기 ③읽고 답하기 ④쓰기로 진행됩니다. 레슨 내용은 목차에 나와 있으며 초급자는 1번 레슨부터 시작하도록 하고 중급자는 자기가 원하는 레슨을 선택해서 수강해도 무방합니다. 각 레슨 진행방식은 아래 설명을 참고하시기 바랍니다.

① GRAMMAR EXERCISE (LEFT-HAND PAGE)

일단 빈칸만 채운다

뉴욕 그래머스쿨의 ①문법학습은 설명이 필요 없을 정도로 쉽고 직관적인 예문 형식으로 구성되어 있습니다. 선생님은 여러분에게 빈 칸이 있는 **미완성 상태의 문장**을 제시합니다. 당신은 이미 완성되어 있는 두 개의 답안을 보고 그것을 응용하여 **빈 칸을 채우기만 하면 됩니다.** 문법은 장황하고 자세한 설명보다 한 줄의 예문을 읽는 것이 훨씬 효과적으로 배울 수 있다는 것이 본 스쿨의 교육 철학입니다.

만약 모르는 문제가 있으면 ②듣고 말하기 레슨에서 선생님이 읽어주는 완전한 문장을 듣고 답을 확인할 수 있습니다.

② HEARING & SPEAKING (RIGHT-HAND PAGE)

선생님은 영어로 질문하고 당신은 영어로 답한다

①문법학습을 통해 완성한 문장을 선생님과 함께 읽어보는 수업입니다. 선생님은 때로는 질문을 하기도 하는데, 당신은 그 **질문에 대해 완전한 문장**full & complete sentence**으로 답변**을 해야 합니다. 그 문장은 ①문법학습의 답이기도 하므로 여러분은 쉽게 답변할 수 있을 것입니다. 대부분의 신입생들이 아직 말하기에 익숙하지 않은 관계로 선생님은 **한 단어씩, 혹은 의미단위로 끊어서 질문**을 합니다. 그 질문에 답변을 하는 사이에 문법이 문장으로 변해 입으로 나오게 될 것입니다. 본 스쿨에서는 말하는 속도나 발음은 평가하지 않습니다. 답을 적어두고 읽거나 천천히 한 단어씩 답해도 무방합니다.

③ READING COMPREHENSION

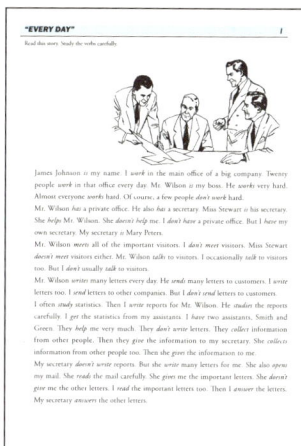
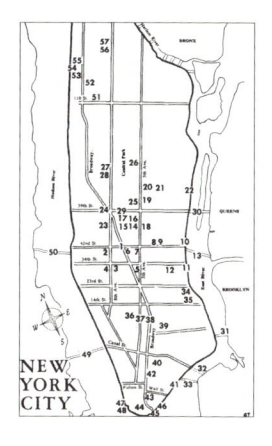
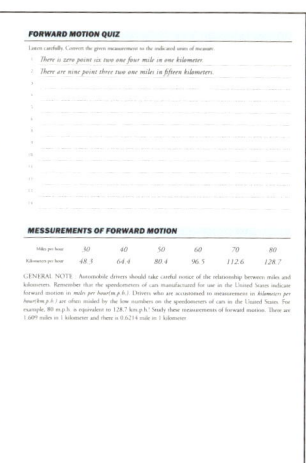

긴 글과 그림 속에 있는 정보를 바탕으로 질문에 답한다

간단한 문장으로 이루어진 글을 읽거나 **그림을 보고 그 안에 들어 있는 정보**나 문법사항을 체크했다가 질문에 답하는 **이해력 수업**입니다. 선생님은 예문을 한 단어씩, 혹은 의미단위로 천천히 여러번 읽어주며 여러분은 그 속에 들어 있는 핵심내용을 오른쪽 페이지에 적어두었다가 선생님의 구두 질문에 완전한 문장으로 답해야 합니다.

④ CURSIVE WRITING PRACTICE

필기체

뉴욕 그래머스쿨은 필기체 쓰기 과정을 정규코스로 채택하고 있습니다. 일상생활 및 비즈니스 현장에서 활자화된 문서 외에 필기체 역시 빈번히 사용되므로 학생 여러**분은 필기체를 자유롭게 읽고 쓸 수 있어야 합니다.**

NEW YORK GRAMMAR SCHOOL CONTENTS 1~59

ELEMENTARY & INTERMEDIATE COURSES

1. EVERY DAY
2. THE SIMPLE PRESENT TENSE
3. THIRD PERSON SINGULAR
4. QUESTIONS AND NEGATIVES
5. DO AND DOES IN QUESTIONS
6. DON'T AND DOESN'T IN NEGATIVES
7. RIGHT NOW
8. THE VERBS AM, IS, AND ARE
9. THE CONTINUOUS PRESENT TENSE
10. QUESTIONS AND NEGATIVES
11. PRESENT TENS NEGATIVE FORMS
12. PRESENT TENSE QUESTION FORMS
13. SIMPLE PRESENT vs CONTINUOUS PRESENT
14. THE WORDS THIS, THESE, THAT, THOSE
15. THE EXPRESSIONS THERE IS AND THERE ARE
16. SUBJECT AND OBJECT PRONOUNS
17. THE POSSESSIVE ENDINGS
18. SHOWING POSSESSION
19. THE POSSESSIVE ADJECTIVES
20. THE POSSESSIVE PRONOUNS
21. FOLLOWING DIRECTIONS
22. GIVING DIRECTIONS
23. POLITE REQUESTS
24. NEGATIVE ORDERS AND REQUESTS
25. SUGGESTIONS WITH LET'S

THE PAST TENSE OF BE	26
THE PAST TENSE OF REGULAR VERBS	27
THE PAST TENSE OF IRREGULAR VERBS	28
REVIEW OF THE PAST TENSE	29
QUESTIONS IN THE PAST TENSE	30
NEGATIVES IN THE PAST TENSE	31
THE BROWNS' TRIP	32
THE PHOTOGRAPHER	33
THE PARTY	34
MY BAD DAY	35
QUESTIONS ABOUT "THE BROWN'S TRIP"	36
QUESTIONS ABOUT "THE PHOTOGRAPHER"	37
QUESTIONS ABOUT "THE PARTY"	38
QUESTIONS ABOUT "MY BAD DAY"	39
IRREGULAR VERB QUIZ(1)	40
IRREGULAR VERB QUIZ(2)	41
IRREGULAR VERB QUIZ(3)	42
IRREGULAR VERB QUIZ(4)	43
IRREGULAR VERB QUIZ(5)	44
IRREGULAR VERB QUIZ(6)	45
REVIEW : QUESTIONS WITH BE	46
REVIEW : QUESTIONS WITH DO	47
THE FUTURE TENSE WITH WILL	48
USING THE FUTURE TENSE(1)	49
THE FUTURE TENSE WITH GO	50
USING THE FUTURE TENSE(2)	51
QUESTIONS : THE FUTURE WITH WILL	52
QUESTIONS : THE FUTURE WITH GO	53
NEGATIVES : THE FUTURE WITH WILL	54
NEGATIVES : THE FUTURE WITH GO	55
USING THE FUTURE TENSES(3)	56
USING THE FUTURE TENSES(4)	57
A TRIP TO NEW YORK	58
QUESTIONS ABOUT "A TRIP TO NEW YORK"	59

NEW YORK GRAMMAR SCHOOL CONTENTS 60-126

60 MUCH. MANY, AND VERY(1)
61 MUCH, MANY, AND VERY(2)
62 A LOT OF AND LOTS OF
63 TOO, TOO MUCH, AND TOO MANY
64 THE WORDS SOME AND ANY
65 SOMETHING vs ANYTHING
66 SOMEONE vs ANYONE
67 ANYONE vs NO ONE
68 DIRECT AND INDIRECT OBJECTS
69 REVIEW : THE PRESENT TENSES
70 REVIEW : QUESTIONS WITH BE AND WILL
71 REVIEW : QUESTIONS WITH DO
72 REVIEW : WRITING QUESTIONS
73 REVIEW : WRITING NEGATIVES
74 SHORT ANSWERS TO QUESTIONS
75 WILLIAM HOWARD HOLT
76 QUESTIONS ABOUT MR. HOLT'S LIFE
77 QUESTIONS ABOUT YOUR ENGLISH CLASS
78 QUESTIONS ABOUT YOUR LIFE
79 USING THE QUESTION WORDS(1)
80 WRITING QUESTIONS WITH WHY
81 THE EXECUTIVE'S DAY
82 QUESTIONS ABOUT "THE EXECUTIVE'S DAY"
83 WHO, WHOM, WHOSE, WHAT, WHICH
84 QUESTIONS WITH HOW
85 ADJECTIVES WITH HOW
86 MUCH AND MANY WITH HOW
87 USING THE QUESTION WORDS(2)
88 USING THE QUESTION WORDS(3)
89 ASKING FOR INFORMATION(1)
90 ASKING FOR INFORMATION(2)
91 NEGATIVE QUESTIONS
92 NEGATIVE QUESTIONS WITH WHY
93 THE PERFECT PRESENT TENSE(1)

THE PERFECT PRESENT TENSE(2)	94
ASKING QUESTIONS	95
MAKING NEGATIVES	96
REVIEW : TENSE FORMS	97
USING IRREGULAR VERBS	98
PERFECT PRESENT vs SIMPLE PAST	99
THE PRESENT TENSES	100
ANSWER PRESUMING QUESTIONS	101
SPECIAL EXPRESSIONS OF TIME	102
EXPRESSIONS OF TIME(1)	103
EXPRESSIONS OF TIME(2)	104
REVIEW : EXPRESSIONS OF TIME	105
EXPRESSIONS OF TIME(3)	106
EXPRESSIONS OF TIME(4)	107
EXPRESSIONS OF TIME(5)	108
REVIEW : EXPRESSIONS OF TIME	109
REVIEW : EXPRESSIONS OF TIME	110
A BRIEF HISTORY OF A.F. ROSSI	111
REVIEW : VERB FORMS	112
REVIEW : QUESTION FORMS	113
EXPRESSIONS OF PLACE	114
VERBS WITH ALLIED PREPOSITIONS	115
ADJECTIVES WITH ALLIED PREPOSITIONS	116
THE WORDS STILL AND ANY MORE	117
THE WORDS ALREADY AND YET	118
REVIEW : STILL, ALREADY, AND YET	119
THE WORDS ALSO, TOO, AND EITHER	120
USING CONTRACTIONS	121
WORD ORDER : FREQUENCY WORDS	122
WORD ORDER : REVIEW	123
WORD ORDER : "PLACE," "MANNER," AND "TIME"	124
WORD ORDER : DIRECT OBJECTS	125
WORD ORDER : DIRECT AND INDIRECT OBJECTS	126

APPENDIX

CURSIVE & FREE WRITING PRACTICE CONTENTS

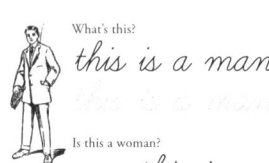

What's this?
this is a man.

Is this a woman?
no, this is not a woman.

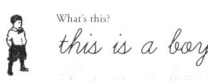

Practice Big!
H H
h h

PAGE

30	CURSIVE WRITING PRACTICE(1)
31	CURSIVE WRITING PRACTICE(2)
42	CURSIVE WRITING PRACTICE(3)
43	CURSIVE WRITING PRACTICE(4)
52	CURSIVE WRITING PRACTICE(5)
53	CURSIVE WRITING PRACTICE(6)
60	CURSIVE WRITING PRACTICE(7)
61	FREE WRITING PRACTICE(1)
74	FREE WRITING PRACTICE(2)
75	FREE WRITING PRACTICE(3)
94	FREE WRITING PRACTICE(4)
95	FREE WRITING PRACTICE(5)
110	FREE WRITING PRACTICE(6)
111	FREE WRITING PRACTICE(7)
122	FREE WRITING PRACTICE(8)
123	FREE WRITING PRACTICE(9)
144	FREE WRITING PRACTICE(10)
145	FREE WRITING PRACTICE(11)
152	FREE WRITING PRACTICE(12)
153	FREE WRITING PRACTICE(13)
167	FREE WRITING PRACTICE(14)
168	FREE WRITING PRACTICE(15)
182	FREE WRITING PRACTICE(16)
183	FREE WRITING PRACTICE(17)
198	FREE WRITING PRACTICE(18)
199	FREE WRITING PRACTICE(19)

What's this?
this is a boy.

What is he doing?
he is pulling the table.

What is he doing?
he is pushing the chair.

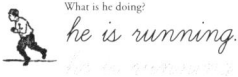

What is he doing?
he is running.

STUDY PLAN SHEET

Lesson	Date	Lesson	Date	Lesson	Date	Lesson	Date
1	. .	34	. .	67	. .	100	. .
2	. .	35	. .	68	. .	101	. .
3	. .	36	. .	69	. .	102	. .
4	. .	37	. .	70	. .	103	. .
5	. .	38	. .	71	. .	104	. .
6	. .	39	. .	72	. .	105	. .
7	. .	40	. .	73	. .	106	. .
8	. .	41	. .	74	. .	107	. .
9	. .	42	. .	75	. .	108	. .
10	. .	43	. .	76	. .	109	. .
11	. .	44	. .	77	. .	110	. .
12	. .	45	. .	78	. .	111	. .
13	. .	46	. .	79	. .	112	. .
14	. .	47	. .	80	. .	113	. .
15	. .	48	. .	81	. .	114	. .
16	. .	49	. .	82	. .	115	. .
17	. .	50	. .	83	. .	116	. .
18	. .	51	. .	84	. .	117	. .
19	. .	52	. .	85	. .	118	. .
20	. .	53	. .	86	. .	119	. .
21	. .	54	. .	87	. .	120	. .
22	. .	55	. .	88	. .	121	. .
23	. .	56	. .	89	. .	122	. .
24	. .	57	. .	90	. .	123	. .
25	. .	58	. .	91	. .	124	. .
26	. .	59	. .	92	. .	125	. .
27	. .	60	. .	93	. .	126	. .
28	. .	61	. .	94	. .		
29	. .	62	. .	95	. .		
30	. .	63	. .	96	. .		
31	. .	64	. .	97	. .		
32	. .	65	. .	98	. .		
33	. .	66	. .	99	. .		

"Perstare et praestare"
To persevere and to excel
인내하라 그리고 탁월해져라

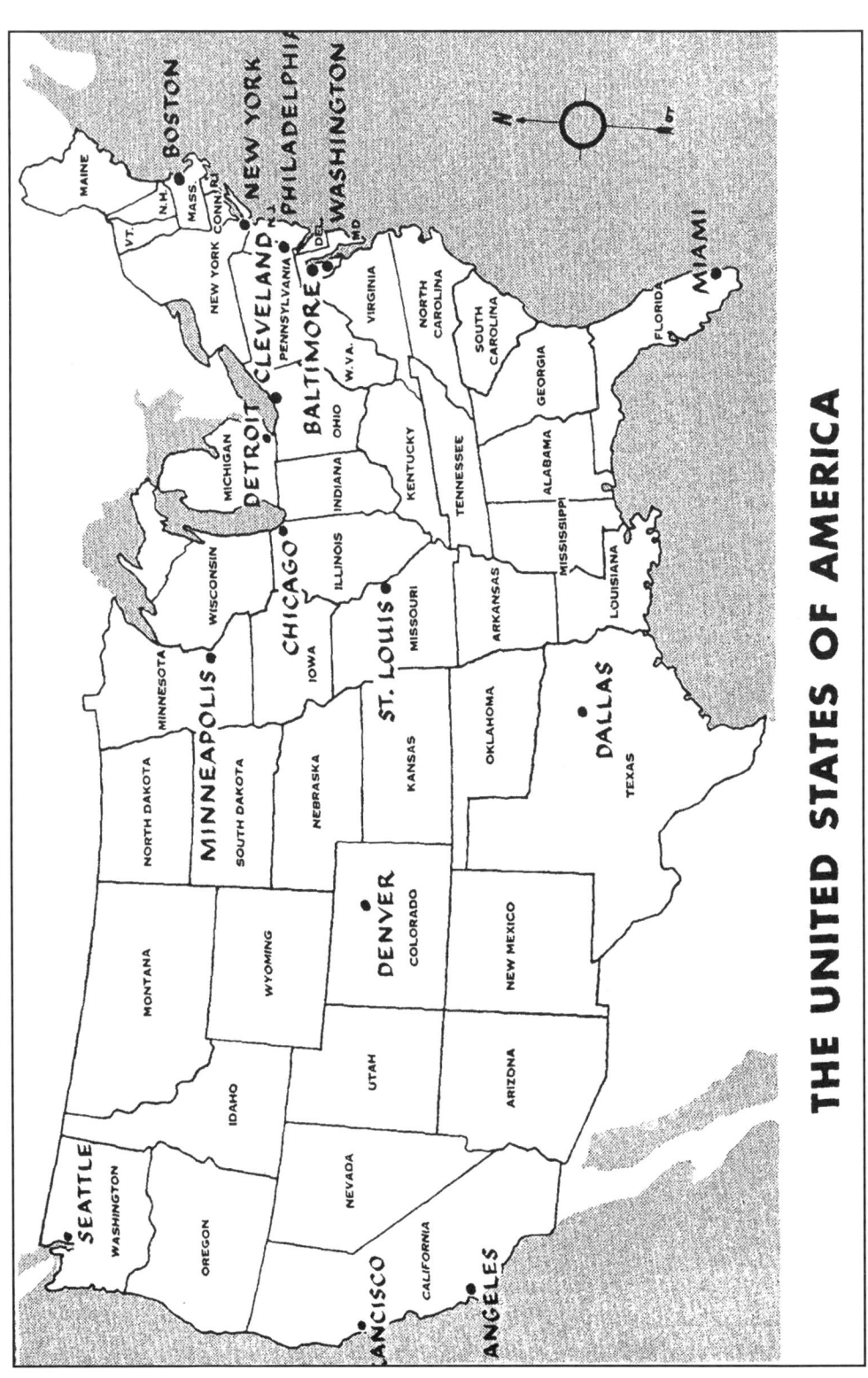

THE 50 STATES OF THE UNITED STATES AND THEIR CAPITALS 🔊

	STATE	CAPITAL		STATE	CAPITAL
1	Alabama(Ala.)	*Montgomery*	26	Montana(Mont.)	*Helena*
2	Alaska(Ak.)	*Junea*	27	Nebraska(Neb.)	*Lincoln*
3	Arizona(Ariz.)	*Phoenix*	28	Nevada(Nev.)	*Carson City*
4	Arkansas(Ark.)	*Little Rock*	29	New Hampshire(N. H.)	*Concord*
5	California(Calif.)	*Sacramento*	30	New Jersey(N. J.)	*Trenton*
6	Colorado(Colo.)	*Denver*	31	New Mexico(N. M.)	*Santa Fe*
7	Connecticut(Conn.)	*Hartford*	32	New York(N. Y.)	*Albany*
8	Delaware(Del.)	*Dover*	33	North Carolina(N. C.)	*Raleigh*
9	Florida(Fla.)	*Tallahassee*	34	North Dakota (N. D.)	*Bismarck*
10	Georgia(Ga.)	*Atlanta*	35	Ohio	*Columbus*
11	Hawaii(Hi.)	*Honolulu*	36	Oklahoma(Okla.)	*Oklahoma City*
12	Idaho	*Boise*	37	Oregon(Ore.)	*Salem*
13	Illinois(Ill.)	*Springfield*	38	Pennsylvania(Pa.)	*Harrisburg*
14	Indiana(Ind.)	*Indianapolis*	39	Rhode Island(R. I.)	*Providence*
15	Iowa	*Des Moines*	40	South Carolina(S. C.)	*Columbia*
16	Kansas(Kans.)	*Topeka*	41	South Dakota(S. D.)	*Pierre*
17	Kentucky(Ky.)	*Frankfort*	42	Tennessee(Tenn.)	*Nashville*
18	Louisiana(La.)	*Baton Rouge*	43	Texas(Tex.)	*Austin*
19	Maine(Me.)	*Augusta*	44	Utah	*Salt Lake City*
20	Maryland(Md.)	*Annapolis*	45	Vermont(Vt.)	*Montpelier*
21	Massachusetts(Mass.)	*Boston*	46	Virginia(Va.)	*Richmond*
22	Michigan(Mich.)	*Lansing*	47	Washington(Wash.)	*Olympia*
23	Minnesota(Minn.)	*St. Paul*	48	West Virginia(W. Va.)	*Charleston*
24	Mississippi(Miss.)	*Jackson*	49	Wisconsin(Wis.)	*Madison*
25	Missouri(Mo.)	*Jefferson City*	50	Wyoming(Wyo.)	*Cheyenne*

GENERAL NOTE : Washington D.C. is the capital of the United States. This city was founded in 1791 to serve as the new national capital and named in honor of George Washington. We call Washington D.C. formally "the District of Columbia" and commonly "Washington", "the District", or simply "D.C."

"EVERY DAY"

Read this story. Study the verbs carefully.

James Johnson *is* my name. I *work* in the main office of a big company. Twenty people *work* in that office every day. Mr. Wilson *is* my boss. He *works* very hard. Almost everyone *works* hard. Of course, a few people *don't work* hard.

Mr. Wilson *has* a private office. He also *has* a secretary. Miss Stewart *is* his secretary. She *helps* Mr. Wilson. She *doesn't help* me. I *don't have* a private office. But I *have* my own secretary. My secretary *is* Mary Peters.

Mr. Wilson *meets* all of the important visitors. I *don't meet* visitors. Miss Stewart *doesn't meet* visitors either. Mr. Wilson *talks* to visitors. I occasionally *talk* to visitors too. But I *don't* usually *talk* to visitors.

Mr. Wilson *writes* many letters every day. He *sends* many letters to customers. I *write* letters too. I *send* letters to other companies. But I *don't send* letters to customers.

I often *study* statistics. Then I *write* reports for Mr. Wilson. He *studies* the reports carefully. I *get* the statistics from my assistants. I *have* two assistants, Smith and Green. They *help* me very much. They *don't write* letters. They *collect* information from other people. Then they *give* the information to my secretary. She *collects* information from other people too. Then she *gives* the information to me.

My secretary *doesn't write* reports. But she *write* many letters for me. She also *opens* my mail. She *reads* the mail carefully. She *gives* me the important letters. She *doesn't give* me the other letters. I *read* the important letters too. Then I *answer* the letters. My secretary *answers* the other letters.

HEARING AND SPEAKING LESSON | 1

Listen carefully. Write all the verbs and read it again.

THE SIMPLE PRESENT TENSE

Use the simple present tense of each verb. Write the verb in the blank space.

1. (work)   I _work_ in the main office.
2. (work)   Mr. Wilson _works_ very hard.
3. (work)   Almost everyone ---- very hard.
4. (work)   We ---- from 9:00 a.m. to 5:00 p.m.
5. (have)   Mr. Wilson ---- a private office.
6. (have)   I ---- my own secretary.
7. (write)   Miss Peters ---- letters for me.
8. (write)   I ---- reports for Mr. Wilson.
9. (study)   Mr. Wilson ---- the reports.
10. (study) I ---- the information carefully.
11. (read)   My secretary ---- all of the mail.
12. (read)   I ---- only the important letters.
13. (collect) Smith and Green ---- information.
14. (collect) Miss Peters ---- information too.

THIRD PERSON SINGULAR

Change the word "I" to "He" or "She." Notice the examples.

1. I go to the office every day.
   —_He goes to the office every day._
2. I write many letters every day.
   —_He writes many letters every day._
3. I read all of the important letters.
4. I study the reports very carefully.
5. I have a private secretary too.
6. I usually work in the main office.
7. I meet all of the important visitors.
8. I get the information from Miss Peters.
9. I always give the reports to Mr. Wilson.
10. I answer all of the important letters.
11. I send letters to many other companies.
12. I talk to Smith and Brown every day.

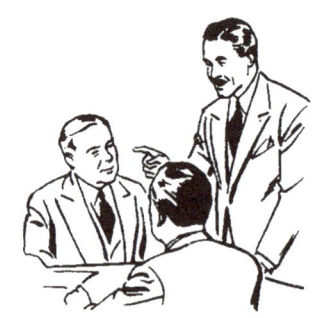

HEARING AND SPEAKING LESSON 2

Listen carefully. Answer the questions with a full sentence.
1. *I work in the main office.*
2. *Mr. Wilson works very hard.*
3.
4.
5.
6.
7.
8.
9.
10.
11.
12.
13.
14.

HEARING AND SPEAKING LESSON 3

Listen carefully. Answer the questions with a full sentence.
1. *He goes to the office every day.*
2. *He writes many letters every day.*
3.
4.
5.
6.
7.
8.
9.
10.
11.
12.

QUESTIONS AND NEGATIVES 4

Answer these questions about the story "Every Day." Answer the questions with a full sentence.

1. Does Mr. Johnson work for a big company?
   —*Yes, Mr. Johnson works for a big company.*
2. Do the two men work in the same room?
   —*No, the two men don't work in the same room.*
3. Does Mr. Johnson have a private office?
4. Do the two men have secretaries?
5. Does Miss Stewart help Mr. Johnson?
6. Does she help Mr. Wilson or Mr. Johnson?
7. Do Mr. Wilson and Mr. Johnson work hard?
8. Does Mr. Wilson meet the important visitors?
9. Does Mr. Johnson talk to the visitors too?
10. Do Mr. Wilson and Mr. Johnson write many letters?
11. Do the two secretaries write letters too?
12. Does Mr. Johnson send letters to customers?
13. Do Mr. Wilson and Mr. Johnson write reports?
14. Does Mr. Wilson study the reports carefully?
15. Does Mr. Johnson study the statistics carefully?
16. Does Mr. Johnson have two assistants?
17. Do Smith and Green give the information to Mr. Johnson?
18. Do they give the information to his secretary?
19. Does Miss Peters give the information to her boss?
20. Does she give the information to Mr. Wilson or Mr. Johnson?
21. Does Miss Peters write reports every day?
22. Do Smith and Green write reports too?
23. Does Mr. Johnson open the mail every day?
24. Does Miss Peters open all of the mail?
25. Do Smith and Green open the mail too?
26. Does Mr. Johnson read all of the mail?
27. Does Mr. Johnson answer all of the letters?
28. Does Mr. Johnson answer only the important letters?

HEARING AND SPEAKING LESSON   4

Answer these questions about the story "Every Day." Answer the questions with a full sentence.

1. *Yes, Mr. Johnson works for a big company.*
2. *No, the two men don't work in the same room.*
3.
4.
5.
6.
7.
8.
9.
10.
11.
12.
13.
14.
15.
16.
17.
18.
19.
20.
21.
22.
23.
24.
25.
26.
27.
28.

DO AND DOES IN QUESTIONS 5

Write *do* or *does* in the blank space in each sentence.

1. *Do* the students study hard every day?
2. *Does* Mr. Brown go to his office every day?
3. ---- you want cream and sugar in your coffee?
4. ---- the children go to bed very early?
5. ---- that girl come from South America?
6. ---- you know that Italian student?
7. ---- Miss Stewart prefer coffee or tea?
8. ---- your English lessons seem very difficult?
9. ---- you have a good English dictionary?
10. ---- Mr. Moore teach English or history?
11. ---- the Johnsons watch television every night?
12. ---- Mr. Johnson and Mr. Wilson work in the same office?
13. ---- you write reports for your boss every day?
14. ---- those two women understand that lesson?

DON'T AND DOESN'T IN NEGATIVES 6

Write *don't* or *doesn't* in the blank space in each sentence.

1. We ---- listen to the radio every night.
2. Mr. Johnson ---- have a private office.
3. The boys ---- study at the library every day.
4. These exercises ---- seem very difficult.
5. It ---- rain very much in June and July.
6. The men ---- always eat at that cafeteria.
7. I ---- eat at that cafeteria every day.
8. Miss Peters ---- write reports for her boss.
9. The Wilsons ---- watch television every night.
10. Smith and Green ---- teach English at this school.
11. That tall man ---- work for this company.
12. The people ---- speak English very well.
13. Mrs. Moore ---- go to the store every day.
14. Miss Graniero ---- enjoy that history class.

HEARING AND SPEAKING LESSON 5

Listen carefully. Answer the questions with a full sentence.

1. *Do the students study hard every day?*
2. *Does Mr. Brown go to his office every day?*
3.
4.
5.
6.
7.
8.
9.
10.
11.
12.
13.
14.

HEARING AND SPEAKING LESSON 6

Listen carefully. Answer the questions with a full sentence.

1. *We don't listen to the radio every night.*
2. *Mr. Johnson Doesn't have a private office.*
3.
4.
5.
6.
7.
8.
9.
10.
11.
12.
13.
14.

CURSIVE WRITING PRACTICE(1)

Practice Big!

Practice Big!

Practice Big!

Practice Big!

CURSIVE WRITING PRACTICE(2)

Practice Big!

$E\ E$

$\ell\ \ell$

Practice Big!

$J\ J$

$f\ f$

Practice Big!

$G\ G$

$g\ g$

Practice Big!

$H\ H$

$h\ h$

"RIGHT NOW" 🔊

Read this story. Study the *verbs* carefully.

My name *is* James Johnson. I *am* the office manager of the Ajax Company. I *am* in the office of the company now. I *am sitting* at my desk right now.

I *am working* on a report for Mr. Wilson. He *is* my boss. Miss Peters *is helping* me with the report. She *is* my secretary. She *is sitting* beside my desk. But she *isn't writing* in her notebook. I *am not dictating* to her at this moment. We *are not working*. We *are resting* for a few minutes. I *am looking* around the office right now.

Mr. Wilson *isn't working* in his office. I *see* four people at the end of the room. Mr. Wilson *is* with the people. He *is taking* the people through our office. He *is telling* the people about our methods. They *are listening* to Mr. Wilson carefully.

Miss Stewart *is wearing* a blue dress today. She *is sitting* at her desk. She *is talking* over the telephone. She *is writing* in her notebook at the same time. Someone *is giving* important information to her over the telephone right now.

There *are* twenty people in the room. Everyone *is working* hard right now. Three or four people *are writing* letters. Some people *are studying* important papers. Smith and Green *are not* here right now. They *are not writing* reports. They *are collecting* information for me.

I *hear* some noise in the hall. There *are* three workers there. The three men *are fixing* the floor in the hall. They *are talking* and laughing. They *are also hitting* the floor with hammers.

HEARING AND SPEAKING LESSON

Listen carefully. Write all the verbs and read it again.

THE VERBS AM, IS, AND ARE   8

Write *am*, *is*, or *are* in the blank space in each sentence.

1. Mr. Wilson *is* talking to visitors right now.
2. I *am* sitting at my desk right at this moment.
3. Miss Peters ---- helping me with a report now.
4. We ---- working on the report right now.
5. I ---- looking around the office at this moment.
6. The people ---- listening to Mr. Wilson carefully.
7. He ---- telling the people about our methods.
8. Someone ---- talking to Miss Stewart right now.
9. She ---- talking and writing at the same time.
10. Everyone ---- working very hard right now.
11. Some people ---- studying important papers now.
12. Smith and Green ---- collecting information now.
13. The men ---- fixing the floor in the hall right now.
14. They ---- also making much noise at this moment.

THE CONTINUOUS PRESENT TENSE   9

Use the continuous present tense of each verb. Write the verb in the blank space.

1. (work)   He *is working* on a report right now.
2. (study) We *are studying* some important papers.
3. (help)   She ---- me with the report now.
4. (sit)   The men ---- at their desks now.
5. (write) The two girls ---- letters now.
6. (work)   Everyone ---- very hard right now.
7. (watch) I ---- my boss and the visitors.
8. (listen) They ---- to Mr. Wilson carefully.
9. (talk)   Someone ---- to Miss Stewart now.
10. (dictate) Mr. Adams ---- letters right now.
11. (collect) Smith and Green ---- information.
12. (talk)
    (write) She ---- and ----- at the same time.
13. (talk)
    (laugh) The men ---- and ---- right now.

HEARING AND SPEAKING LESSON 🔊 8

Listen carefully. Answer the questions with a full sentence.

1. *Mr. Wilson is talking to visitors right now.*
2. *I am sitting at my desk right at this moment.*
3.
4.
5.
6.
7.
8.
9.
10.
11.
12.
13.
14.

HEARING AND SPEAKING LESSON 🔊 9

Listen carefully. Answer the questions with a full sentence.

1. *He is working on a report right now.*
2. *We are studying some important papers.*
3.
4.
5.
6.
7.
8.
9.
10.
11.
12.
13.

QUESTIONS AND NEGATIVES   10

Answer these questions about the story "Right Now." Answer the questions with a complete sentence.

1. Is Mr. Johnson the office manager?
   —<u>Yes, Mr. Johnson is the office manager.</u>
2. Is Mr. Wilson in his private office now?
   —<u>No, Mr. Wilson isn't in his private office now.</u>
3. Is Mr. Johnson sitting at his desk right now?
   —<u>Yes, Mr. Johnson is sitting at his desk right now.</u>
4. Is Mr. Wilson working on a report at the moment?
   —<u>No, Mr. Wilson isn't working on a report at the moment.</u>

5. Is Miss Peters helping Mr. Johnson right now?
6. Is Miss Peters sitting at her own desk now?
7. Is Mr. Johnson dictating to Miss Peters now?
8. Is Miss Peters writing in her notebook right now?
9. Are Mr. Johnson and Miss Peters working on a report?
10. Are they working on the report right at this moment?
11. Are they resting for a few minutes?
12. Is Mr. Johnson looking around the office now?
13. Is Mr. Wilson in his private office right now?
14. Does Mr. Johnson see many people in the office?
15. Are the four customers with Mr. Wilson now?
16. Is Mr. Wilson with the four visitors now?
17. Is Mr. Wilson talking to the four people right now?
18. Are the people listening to Mr. Wilson carefully?
19. Is Miss Stewart sitting beside Mr. Johnson right now?
20. Is Miss Stewart talking to someone at this moment?
21. Are there very many people in the office now?
22. Are Smith and Green in the main office now?
23. Are Smith and Green helping Mr. Johnson now?
24. Does Mr. Johnson hear noise in the hall now?
25. Are the three workers talking and laughing?
26. Are they also hitting the floor with hammers?

HEARING AND SPEAKING LESSON

10

Answer these questions about the story "Right Now." Answer the questions with a complete sentence.

1. *Yes, Mr. Johnson is the office manager.*
2. *No, Mr. Wilson isn't in his private office now.*
3.
4.
5.
6.
7.
8.
9.
10.
11.
12.
13.
14.
15.
16.
17.
18.
19.
20.
21.
22.
23.
24.
25.
26.

PRESENT TENS NEGATIVE FORMS   11

Write *don't, doesn't, isn't, aren't,* or *am not* in the blank space in each sentence.

1. He *isn't* listening to the radio right now.
2. He *doesn't* listen to the radio every evening.
3. We ---- watching a television program now.
4. We ---- watch television every day.
5. They ---- study their lessons after class.
6. They ---- studying their lessons right now.
7. It ---- raining very hard right at the moment.
8. It ---- rain very much during the summer.
9. Mr. Johnson ---- eating his lunch now.
10. Mr. Johnson ---- always eat at that place.
11. I ---- see any students in that room.
12. I ---- hear anyone in the hall now.
13. They ---- like milk with their meals.
14. They ---- have enough money for a new car.

PRESENT TENSE QUESTION FORMS   12

Write *do, does, is, are,* or *am* in the blank space in each sentence.

1. *Do* the men come to work at 9:00 every morning?
2. *Are* the men coming into the room right now?
3. ---- you learn the new words in each lesson?
4. ---- you learning the new words right now?
5. ---- Mr. Johnson work for the Ajax Company?
6. ---- Mr. Johnson working on a report right now?
7. ---- she usually sit in the third row?
8. ---- she sitting in the fourth row today?
9. ---- you read many books every year?
10. ---- you reading an interesting book now?
11. ---- the students need help with their lessons?
12. ---- this lesson seem very difficult to you?
13. ---- you remember the name of that book?
14. ---- you understand all of the words very well?

HEARING AND SPEAKING LESSON 11

Listen carefully. Answer the questions with a full sentence.

1. *He isn't listening to the radio right now.*
2. *He doesn't listen to the radio every evening.*
3.
4.
5.
6.
7.
8.
9.
10.
11.
12.
13.
14.

HEARING AND SPEAKING LESSON 12

Listen carefully. Answer the questions with a full sentence.

1. *Do the men come to work at 9:00 every morning?*
2. *Are the men coming into the room right now?*
3.
4.
5.
6.
7.
8.
9.
10.
11.
12.
13.
14.

SIMPLE PRESENT vs CONTINUOUS PRESENT 13

Use the correct tense of the verb in each sentence. Choose between the simple present tense and the continuous present tense.

1. He (*work*) hard every day. —*He works hard every day.*
2. He (*talk*) to Tom now. —*He is talking to Tom now.*
3. Miss Stewart (*look*) at the newspaper now.
4. The children (*sleep*) for two hours every afternoon.
5. Those two fellows (*fix*) the car right now.
6. That French girl (*speak*) English very well.
7. Uncle Walter (*eat*) dinner with us every Sunday.
8. My friend (*enjoy*) hamburgers very much.
9. John and Frank (*write*) letters at this moment.
10. Mr. Johnson (*work*) thirty-five hours a week.
11. My sister (*need*) some money for her books.
12. It (*rain*) very much in the United States.
13. Mr. Brown (*pay*) his bills once a month.
14. The student (*look up*) that new word right now.
15. Mr. Moore (*teach*) English from 2:00 to 4:00 p.m.
16. Mr. Moore (*begin*) the new lesson right now.
17. I (*owe*) my friend two dollars and fifty cents.
18. Smith (*watch*) a baseball game every Saturday.
19. Miss Peters (*talk*) to Mr. Johnson right now.
20. Pierre (*know*) all of the new words very well now.
21. We always (*do*) our English lessons carefully.
22. We (*do*) exercise thirteen right at the moment.
23. The sun (*get*) very hot during the afternoon.
24. Alice and Mary (*put away*) the dinner dishes right now.
25. Mr. Harris (*read*) an interesting book about Lincoln.
26. The Moores often (*attend*) our Tuesday night meetings.
27. Mr. Berg (*talk*) to his teacher about that mistake.
28. I frequently (*do*) my homework on the bus.
29. I (*do*) the next to last sentence right now.
30. The teacher (*close*) the door at nine o'clock sharp.

HEARING AND SPEAKING LESSON

Listen carefully. Answer the questions with a full sentence.

1. *He works hard every day.*
2. *He is talking to Tom now.*
3.
4.
5.
6.
7.
8.
9.
10.
11.
12.
13.
14.
15.
16.
17.
18.
19.
20.
21.
22.
23.
24.
25.
26.
27.
28.
29.
30.

CURSIVE WRITING PRACTICE(3)

Practice Big!

Practice Big!

Practice Big!

Practice Big!

CURSIVE WRITING PRACTICE(4)

THE WORDS THIS, THESE, THAT, THOSE 14

Choose *this* or *these*.Choose *that* or *those*.

1. *This* is your briefcase.
2. *These* are your books.
3. ---- book is interesting.
4. ---- questions are hard.
5. ---- is very difficult.
6. ---- are quite easy.
7. ---- seem very hard.
8. ---- seems very easy.
9. ---- lesson is simple.
10. ---- words are new.
11. ---- are very heavy.
12. ---- is very pretty.
13. ---- goes on lines.
14. --- go on line.

15. Is *that* man here now?
16. Are *those* students ready?
17. Is ---- your notebook?
18. Are ---- your gloves?
19. Is ---- boy reading now?
20. Are ---- students working?
21. Does ---- seem difficult?
22. Do ---- feel comfortable?
23. Are ---- children here?
24. Do ---- men speak English?
25. Does ---- woman know you?
26. Is ---- lesson very easy?
27. Do ---- belong on ---- desk?
28. Does ---- go in ---- drawers?

THE EXPRESSIONS THERE IS AND THERE ARE 15

Use *there is* and *there are* and *in the room* with these words. Make statements and questions. Notice the examples.

1. a table —*There is a table in the room.*
   —*Is there a table in the room?*
2. chairs —*There are chairs in the room.*
   —*Are there chairs in the room?*

3. a picture
4. desks
5. a blackboard
6. a chair
7. a telephone
8. windows
9. a rug
10. people
11. two doors
12. a closet
13. some men
14. three maps
15. a wastebasket
16. children
17. many chairs
18. an ashtray
19. a big table
20. some women
21. a pretty picture
22. many people
23. a small man
24. four chairs
25. much light
26. many lamps

HEARING AND SPEAKING LESSON 14

Listen carefully. Answer the questions with a full sentence.

1. *This is your book.*
2. *These are your books.*
3.
4.
5.
6.
7.
8.
9.
10.
11.
12.
13.
14.
15.
16.
17.
18.
19.
20.
21.
22.
23.
24.
25.
26.
27.
28.

HEARING AND SPEAKING LESSON 15

Listen carefully. Answer the questions with a full sentence.

3. *There is a picture in the room.*
   Is there a picture in the room?
4. *There are desks in the room.*
   Are there desks in the room?
5.
6.
7.
8.
9.
10.
11.
12.
13.
14.
15.
16.
17.
18.

SUBJECT AND OBJECT PRONOUNS   16

Substitute pronouns for the italicized words in each sentence. Notice the first two examples.

1. *The boy* is reading *the book*. —<u>He is reading it.</u>
2. *The students* are talking to *Tom*. —<u>They are talking to him.</u>
3. *Mary* is studying her lesson with *John*.
4. *Mr. and Mrs. Johnson* enjoy *television* very much.
5. *That fellow* understands *the lesson* completely.
6. *The children* like *their teachers* very much.
7. Do *Charles and Mary* like *that English book*?
8. Is *Miss Brown* explaining the lesson to *the students*?
9. *The women* are talking about *the party*.
10. *The man* is moving *the furniture* into the other room.
11. *Those people* need *the money* as soon as possible.
12. *John and Frank* are writing *the letter* right now.
13. *Frank and I* usually meet *our friends* at the corner.
14. *The two girls* are putting *the food* on the table now.
15. Are *the men* speaking to *Mr. Wilson* at this moment?
16. *The teachers* spoke to *the students* about *that matter*.
17. *John, Frank, and I* are studying *the new words* now.
18. *The waitress* always washes *the tables* carefully.
19. Does *Mrs. Brown* buy *her groceries* at that store?
20. *All of the students* enjoy *baseball* very much.
21. *Betty* sends a letter to *her parents* every week.
22. *Mr. Harris* is helping *that student* with *the lesson*.
23. Do *Bill and you* read *that newspaper* every morning?
24. *The people* don't like *the news* very much.
25. *The student* is writing *the explanation* in his notebook.
26. *The police* protect *the city* day and night.
27. *The police officer* is giving a ticket to *that woman*.
28. *The United States* consists of fifty individual states.
29. *The teacher* is explaining *the words* to *Miss Graniero*.
30. *His friends* always enjoy *his jokes* very much.

HEARING AND SPEAKING LESSON

Listen carefully. Answer the questions with a full sentence.

1. *He is reading it.*
2. *They are talking to him.*
3.
4.
5.
6.
7.
8.
9.
10.
11.
12.
13.
14.
15.
16.
17.
18.
19.
20.
21.
22.
23.
24.
25.
26.
27.
28.
29.
30.

THE POSSESSIVE ENDINGS   17

Write the correct possessive form of each word in parentheses.

1. (*Helen*) hat is pretty. —<u>Helen's hat is pretty.</u>
2. The (*boys*) books are here. —<u>The boys' books are here.</u>
3. (*Frank*) English isn't very good.
4. That (*girl*) summer suit is beautiful.
5. The (*girls*) new apartment is lovely.
6. Mr. (*Brown*) son knows Bill and Tom well.
7. That (*man*) brother works for the Ajax Company.
8. Those (*men*) coats are in the other closet.
9. The (*student*) books are on his desk.
10. The (*students*) papers are in that drawer.
11. (*Tom*) (*friend*) sister lives in San Francisco.
12. (*Fred*) (*parents*) house is at the end of the next block.

SHOWING POSSESSION   18

Show possession with *'s* or *s'* or *of*. Add *the* if necessary. Notice the first two examples.

1. (*man*) (*name*) is unusual. —<u>The man's name is unusual.</u>
2. (*book*) (*title*) is short. —<u>The title of the book is short.</u>
3. (*doctor*) (*office*) is on the tenth floor.
4. (*table*) (*legs*) are not very strong.
5. Does Mr. Johnson know (*price*) (*car*)?
6. Do Alice and Betty know (*boys*) (*friend*)?
7. Does anyone know (*height*) (*that wall*)?
8. (*coats*) (*women*) are in the closet in the hall.
9. (*table*) (*surface*) is not very smooth.
10. (*cover*) (*book*) is yellow and black.
11. The students usually write on (*paper*) (*both sides*).
12. All of our suitcases are in (*trunk*) (*car*).
13. Mr. Harris is talking to (*student*) (*father*).
14. Mrs. Edna Wilson is (*aunt*) (*Miss Stewart*).
15. The two workers are repairing (*house*) (*roof*).
16. (*new car*) (*John*) is certainly very beautiful.

HEARING AND SPEAKING LESSON 17

Listen carefully. Answer the questions with a full sentence.

1 *Helen's hat is pretty.*
2 *The boys' books are here.*
3
4
5
6
7
8
9
10
11
12

HEARING AND SPEAKING LESSON 18

Listen carefully. Answer the questions with a full sentence.

1 *The man's name is unusual.*
2 *The title of the book is short.*
3
4
5
6
7
8
9
10
11
12
13
14
15
16

THE POSSESSIVE ADJECTIVES

Refer to the italicized word or words with the correct possessive adjective. Notice the first two examples.

1. The man is studying *his* English assignment now.
2. Miss Peters is writing in *her* notebook right now.
3. They usually eat ---- lunch at the Ritz Cafeteria.
4. We always study ---- English lessons very carefully.
5. That girl always takes very good care of ---- clothes.
6. The children are playing with ---- toys right now.
7. I always put ---- pens and pencils in the second drawer.
8. You don't do ---- English lessons very carefully.
9. Tom and Bill are walking home with ---- friends.
10. Mr. Brown seldom drives ---- car to ---- office.
11. Miss Davis is using ---- sister's book today.
12. We write letters to ---- friends once or twice a month.
13. Mr. and Mrs. Wilson are sitting in ---- living room now.
14. You and I don't spend ---- money very carefully.

THE POSSESSIVE PRONOUNS

Substitute a possessive pronoun for the words in parentheses in each sentence. Notice the first two examples.

1. That book is (*my book*). —*That book is mine.*
2. Those are (*her pictures*). —*Those are hers.*
3. All of these magazines are (*his magazines*).
4. Those cigarettes on the table are (*my cigarettes*).
5. Are all of these papers (*your papers*)?
6. That newspaper on the desk is (*her newspaper*).
7. That big white house on the corner is (*their house*).
8. Is this your purse or (*Miss Brown's purse*)?
9. Are those my overshoes or (*his overshoes*)?
10. Are these two books (*your books*) or (*my books*)?
11. Edward's new suit and (*my new suit*) are very similar.
12. Their house and (*our house*) are both on the same block.
13. That red car in front of (*your car*) is (*my brother's car*).
14. Is this English book (*your book*) or (*his sister's book*)?

HEARING AND SPEAKING LESSON — 19

Listen carefully. Answer the questions with a full sentence.

1. *The man is studying his English assignment now.*
2. *Miss Peters is writing in her notebook right now.*
3.
4.
5.
6.
7.
8.
9.
10.
11.
12.
13.
14.

HEARING AND SPEAKING LESSON — 20

Listen carefully. Answer the questions with a full sentence.

1. *That book is mine.*
2. *Those are hers.*
3.
4.
5.
6.
7.
8.
9.
10.
11.
12.
13.
14.

CURSIVE WRITING PRACTICE(5)

Practice Big!

2 2

q q

Practice Big!

R R

n n

Practice Big!

S S

s s

Practice Big!

T T

t t

CURSIVE WRITING PRACTICE(6)

Practice Big!

Practice Big!

Practice Big!

Practice Big!

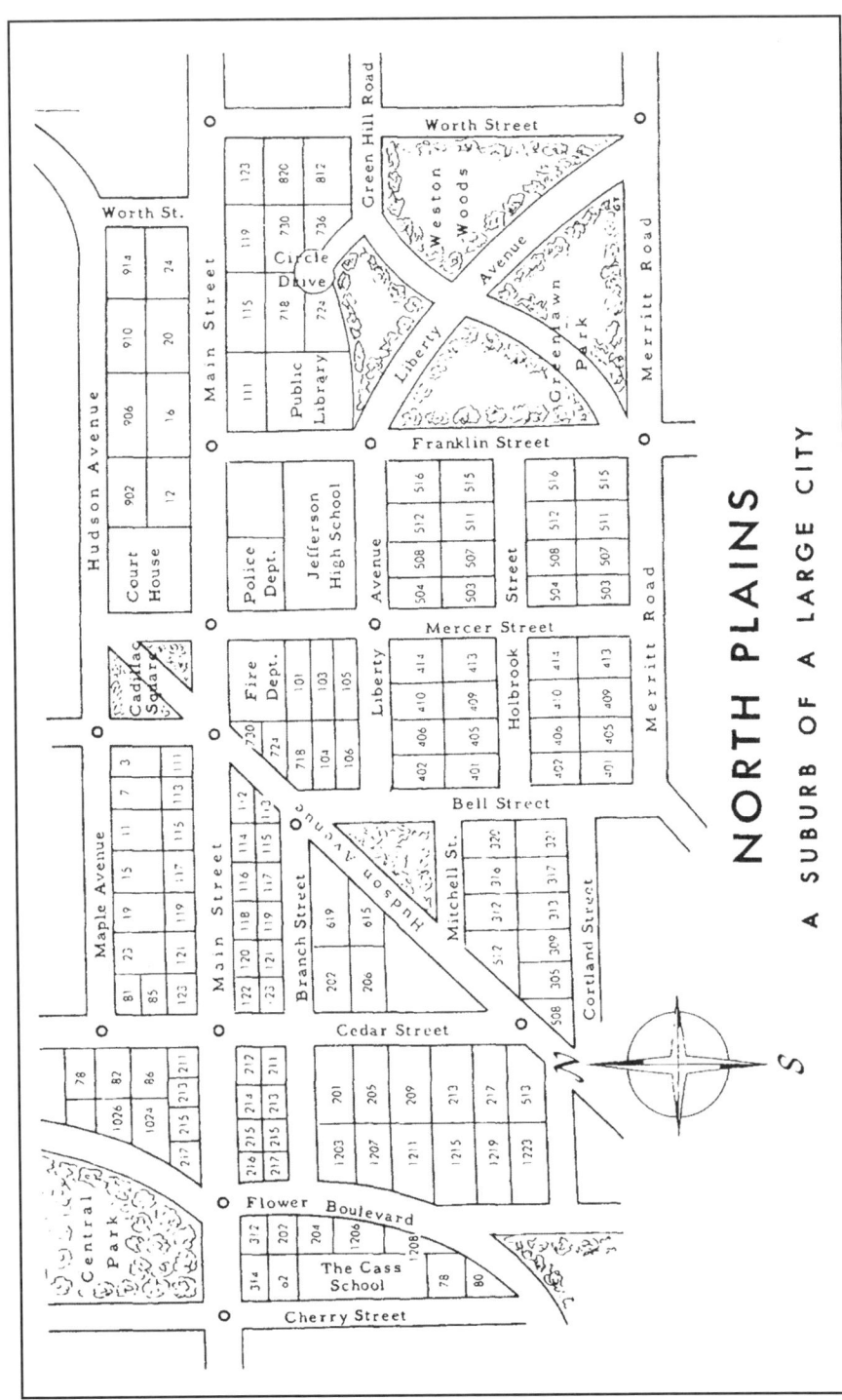

MESSUREMENTS OF FORWARD MOTION

Miles per hour	30	40	50	60	70	80
Kilometers per hour	48.3	64.4	80.4	96.5	112.6	128.7

GENERAL NOTE : Automobile drivers should take careful notice of the relationship between miles and kilometers. Remember that the speedometers of cars manufactured for use in the United States indicate forward motion in *miles per hour(m.p.h.)*. Drivers who are accustomed to measurement in *kilometers per hour(km.p.h.)* are often misled by the low numbers on the speedometers of cars in the United States. For example, 80 m.p.h. is equivalent to 128.7 km.p.h.! Study these measurements of forward motion. There are 1.609 miles in 1 kilometer and there is 0.6214 mile in 1 kilometer.

FORWARD MOTION QUIZ

Listen carefully. Convert the given measurement to the indicated units of measure.

1. *There is zero point six two one four mile in one kilometer.*
2. *There are nine point three two one miles in fifteen kilometers.*
3.
4.
5.
6.
8.
9.
10.
11.
12.
13.
14.

FOLLOWING DIRECTIONS 🔊   21

Follow these directions carefully. Use the map on page 54. Then look in the appendix for the correct address of each location.

1. *Where do Mr. and Mrs. Smith live?*

   You are at the corner of Main Street and Cherry Street. Drive east to the third stop light. Turn right. Turn left at the next light. Drive to Holbrook Street, and turn to your left. Stop at the third house on your right.

2. *Where is the Booth Shoe Store?*

   You are at the corner of Main Street and Worth Street. Walk west to the third stop light. Turn left. Then turn right at the next corner. Go to the third store on your right.

3. *Where do the Browns live?*

   You are in front of Jefferson High School. Drive west on Liberty to Bell. Make a right turn. Cross Hudson Avenue and take Branch Street to Cedar. Turn left on Cedar Street. It's the second house on your left.

4. *Please give me the directions to Mr. Johnson's house.*

   You are at the corner of Bell Street and Cortland Street. Go north on Bell to Liberty Avenue. Make a right turn on Liberty. Take Liberty to Green Hill Road. His house is on the northwest corner of Worth Street and Green Hill Road.

GIVING DIRECTIONS 🔊   22

Give the correct directions for the following places.

1. I'm at the corner of Cedar Street and Branch Street. *Please give me the directions to* <u>Greenlawn Park.</u>
2. I'm at Franklin Street and Merrit Road. *Please direct me to* <u>the Cass School.</u>
3. I'm at the corner of Maple Avenue and Cedar Street. *How do I get to* <u>Jefferson High School?</u>
4. I'm at the corner of Worth Street and Hudson Avenue. *Please give me the directions to* <u>the Public Library.</u>
5. I'm at the corner of Bell Street and Holbrook. *How do I get to* <u>the Court House?</u>
6. I'm at the corner of Merrit Road and Liberty Avenue. *Where is* <u>the North Plains commercial section</u>?

HEARING AND SPEAKING LESSON 21

Listen carefully. Answer the questions with a full sentence.

1. *Where do Mr. and Mrs. Smith live?*
   Mr. ad Mrs. Smith live on 410, Holbrook St.

2. *Where is the Booth Shoe Store?*

3. *Where do the Browns live?*

4. *Please give me the directions to Mr. Johnson's house.*

HEARING AND SPEAKING LESSON 22

Listen carefully. Answer the questions with a full sentence.

1.
2.
3.
4.
5.
6.

POLITE REQUESTS 23

Change these orders and directions to polite requests. Use two forms. Notice the first two examples.

1. Open the door.
   —*Please open the door.*
   —*Would you please open the door?*
2. Come at 7:30.
   —*Please come at 7:30.*
   —*Would you please come at 7:30?*
3. Give me the magazine.
4. Shut that window.
5. Finish your work.
6. Come back soon.
7. Call me before 5:30.
8. Mail the letter today.
9. Pass the sugar.
10. Tell me the answer.
11. Bring it to me.
12. Return those books.

NEGATIVE ORDERS AND REQUESTS 24

Change these orders and directions to polite requests. Use two forms. Notice the first two examples.

1. Shut the door.
   —*Don't shut the door.*
   —*Please don't shut the door.*
2. Sit on the sofa.
   —*Don't sit on the sofa.*
   —*Please don't sit on the sofa.*
3. Put the box there.
4. Move the chairs.
5. Call me after 5:30.
6. Bring your friend today.
7. Tell them about that.
8. Put your coat there.
9. Turn off the light.
10. Turn on the radio.
11. Push the table back.
12. Talk to me now.

SUGGESTIONS WITH LET'S 25

Change these orders and directions to suggestions with *let's*. Write the negative form also. Notice the first two examples.

1. Call Fred tonight.
   —*Let's call Fred tonight.*
   —*Let's not call Fred tonight.*
2. Study that lesson now.
   —*Let's study that lesson now.*
   —*Let's not study that lesson now.*
3. Visit Mr. and Mrs. Moore.
4. Learn those words now.
5. Read the newspaper.
6. Walk to school today.
7. Listen to the radio.
8. See that movie.
9. Watch television tonight.
10. Finish the work now.
11. Go to the store.
12. Study those two lessons.

HEARING AND SPEAKING LESSON 23

Listen carefully. Answer the questions with a full sentence.

1 *Please open the door.*
  Would you please open the door?
2
3
4
5

6
7
8
9
10
11
12

HEARING AND SPEAKING LESSON 24

Listen carefully. Answer the questions with a full sentence.

1 *Don't shut the door.*
  Please don't shut the door.
2
3
4
5

6
7
8
9
10
11
12

HEARING AND SPEAKING LESSON 25

Listen carefully. Answer the questions with a full sentence.

1 *Let's call Fred tonight.*
  Let's not call Fred tonight.
2
3
4
5

6
7
8
9
10
11
12

CURSIVE WRITING PRACTICE(7)

Practice Big!

Practice Big!

FREE WRITING PRACTICE(1)

abcdefghijklmnopqrstuvwxyz
abcdefghijklmnopqrstuvwxyz
abcdefghijklmnopqrstuvwxyz
abcdefghijklmnopqrstuvwxyz
abcdefghijklmnopqrstuvwxyz
abcdefghijklmnopqrstuvwxyz
abcdefghijklmnopqrstuvwxyz
abcdefghijklmnopqrstuvwxyz
abcdefghijklmnopqrstuvwxyz
abcdefghijklmnopqrstuvwxyz
abcdefghijklmnopqrstuvwxyz

THE PAST TENSE OF BE   26

Change the verb in each sentence to the past tense.

1. He *is* in his office.
   —He *was* in his office.
2. We *are* almost ready.
   —We *were* almost ready.
3. You *are* very late.
   —You *were* very late.
4. They *are* at work.
5. It *is* in that drawer.
6. She *is* in New York.
7. I *am* very tired.
8. That *is* a surprise.
9. The men *are* angry.
10. Mr. Harris *is* there.
11. You *are* on time.
12. *Is* the teacher here?
13. *Are* you very tired?
14. *Am* I right or wrong?
15. *Are* the lessons easy?
16. *Is* the sandwich good?
17. *Are* you in that class?
18. *Is* that book interesting?
19. He *is* not in the room.
20. I *am* not very tired.
21. The man *is* not busy.
22. They *are* not hungry.
23. Miss Brown *is* not here.
24. Those *are* not very easy.
25. That *is* not difficult.

THE PAST TENSE OF REGULAR VERBS   27

Use the past tense form of the verb in parentheses in each sentence.

1. We (*finish*) the work yesterday. —*We finished the work yesterday.*
2. Frank (*borrow*) some money from his friend last night.
3. Mr. Harris (*explain*) the lesson to us very carefully.
4. I (*like*) that movie about President Wilson's life.
5. That company (*hire*) twenty new workers last year.
6. The students (*study*) those two lessons yesterday.
7. Everyone (*enjoy*) the party very much last night.
8. The driver (*stop*) the bus very quickly.
9. The clerk (*count*) the money two or three times.
10. My friend (*help*) me with my homework this afternoon.
11. Mr. Berg (*describe*) his trip to us after class yesterday.
12. My sister (*stay*) in Europe for two and a half months.
13. All of the students (*copy*) the assignment carefully.
14. The secretary (*omit*) two or three names from the list.

HEARING AND SPEAKING LESSON 26

Listen carefully. Answer the questions with a full sentence.

1. *He was in his office.*
2. *We were almost ready.*
3.
4.
5.
6.
7.
8.
9.
10.
11.
12.
13.
14.
15.
16.
17.
18.
19.
20.
21.
22.
23.
24.
25.

HEARING AND SPEAKING LESSON 27

Listen carefully. Answer the questions with a full sentence.

1. *We finished the work yesterday.*
2. *Frank borrowed some money from his friend last night.*
3.
4.
5.
6.
7.
8.
9.
10.
11.
12.
13.
14.

THE PAST TENSE OF IRREGULAR VERBS   28

Use the past tense form of the verb in parentheses in each sentence. Check your work with the list of irregular verbs in the appendix.

1. We (*go*) to a concert. —*We went to a concert.*
2. He (*bring*) his friend. —*He brought his friend.*
3. Frank (*take*) a course in French last year.
4. We (*find*) Miss Stewart's purse under a chair.
5. Mr. Berg (*speak*) to the teacher right after class.
6. Mr. Johnson (*put*) all of the papers in his briefcase.
7. You (*make*) several mistakes in the last exercise.
8. I (*drink*) two cups of coffee at breakfast today.
9. Mr. Harris (*tell*) the students the answer to the question.
10. Charles (*leave*) for California three days ago.
11. Mr. and Mrs. Wilson (*sell*) their old house at a low price.
12. The Wilsons (*build*) a new house in North Plains.
13. All of the students (*read*) the assignment carefully.
14. We (*eat*) lunch at the cafeteria with our friends.

REVIEW OF THE PAST TENSE   29

Use the past tense form of the verb in parentheses in each sentence.

1. They (*sell*) their house. —*They sold their house.*
2. They (*walk*) to the corner. *They walked to the corner.*
3. We (*listen*) to that radio program last night.
4. Mr. Johnson (*ride*) downtown with his friend today.
5. The two men (*carry*) the furniture very carefully.
6. Professor Taylor (*teach*) a different class last year.
7. The students (*practice*) the new words after their class.
8. We (*spend*) two and a half weeks in Los Angeles.
9. Everyone in the audience (*enjoy*) the professor's speech.
10. Mr. Wilson (*drive*) his car to work this morning.
11. I (*repeat*) each new word four or five times.
12. The secretary (*put*) the dictionary beside the typewriter.
13. The rain (*stop*) in the middle of the afternoon.
14. The Browns (*receive*) a letter from them several days ago.

HEARING AND SPEAKING LESSON 28

Listen carefully. Answer the questions with a full sentence.

1 *We went to a concert.*
2 *He brought his friend.*
3
4
5
6
7
8
9
10
11
12
13
14

HEARING AND SPEAKING LESSON 29

Listen carefully. Answer the questions with a full sentence.

1 *They sold their house.*
2 *They walked to the corner.*
3
4
5
6
7
8
9
10
11
12
13
14

QUESTIONS IN THE PAST TENSE — 30

Change the following statements to questions. Study the first three examples carefully.

1. They finished the work. —*Did they finish the work?*
2. They spoke to John. —*Did they speak to John?*
3. They were in their office. —*Were they in their office?*
4. Mr. and Mrs. Wilson visited their friends in Detroit.
5. The teacher told the students the answer to the question.
6. That movie about Wilson's life was interesting.
7. Mr. Harris explained the meaning of the word to her.
8. Those men from South America were at the meeting.
9. The students studied carefully for the examination.
10. The Wilsons sold their house at a low price.
11. The last lesson was very difficult for the students.
12. Their friends watched that television program last night.
13. The man read the instructions in the book very carefully.
14. There were many people at the party last Friday night.

NEGATIVES IN THE PAST TENSE — 31

Change the following statements to negatives. Study the first three examples very carefully.

1. He worked very hard. —*He didn't work very hard.*
2. He drove very carefully. —*He didn't drive very carefully.*
3. He was at the meeting. —*He wasn't at the meeting.*
4. The secretary copied the names from the list carefully.
5. Alice ate lunch at the cafeteria with her friends.
6. The students were ready for the examination.
7. Mr. Harris taught at Eastern University last summer.
8. The teacher noticed the mistake in that sentence.
9. The last two lessons were very difficult for me.
10. The students brought their dictionaries to class yesterday.
11. The director agreed with his assistants on that matter.
12. There were many people in the audience last night.
13. Mr. Johnson prepared that report for Mr. Wilson.
14. Our friends went to the movies with us on Saturday night.

HEARING AND SPEAKING LESSON 30

Listen carefully. Answer the questions with a full sentence.

1. *Did they finish the work?*
2. *Did they speak to John?*
3.
4.
5.
6.
7.
8.
9.
10.
11.
12.
13.
14.

HEARING AND SPEAKING LESSON 31

Listen carefully. Answer the questions with a full sentence.

1. *He didn't work very hard.*
2. *He didn't drive very carefully.*
3.
4.
5.
6.
7.
8.
9.
10.
11.
12.
13.
14.

"THE BROWNS' TRIP" 32

Use the past tense form of the verb in parentheses in each sentence.

1. The Browns (*take*) a trip.
2. They (*go*) to South America.
3. First they (*drive*) to Miami.
4. Then they (*fly*) to Havana, Cuba.
5. Next they (*leave*) for Mexico.
6. They (*spend*) two weeks in Mexico.
7. They (*have*) a good time in Bogota.
8. The Browns (*see*) many interesting things in Quito, Ecuador.
9. They (*write*) many letters to their friends from South America.
10. The Browns (*buy*) unusual gifts for their friends in Bolivia.
11. The whole trip (*cost*) the Browns about two thousand dollars.

"THE PHOTOGRAPHER" 33

Use the past tense form of the verb in parentheses in each sentence.

1. Fred (*buy*) a camera from his friend Bill last month.
2. His friend Bill (*sell*) the camera to him for eighty dollars.
3. Fred (*pay*) for the camera in cash.
4. Fred (*know*) almost nothing about photography at the time.
5. Bill (*give*) Fred a book with complete instructions.
6. Fred (*read*) all of the instructions very carefully.
7. Fred (*keep*) the camera in a case for protection.
8. Then Fred (*take*) pictures of all of his friends.
9. Of course, Fred (*hold*) the camera very carefully.
10. Fred (*leave*) the films at a photographic store the next day.
11. Fred (*get*) the pictures back two or three days later.
12. All of the pictures (*come out*) very clearly.
13. Fred (*bring*) all of the pictures to class yesterday.
14. Bill (*see*) all of Fred's photographs.
15. Bill (*say*) all of the pictures were very good.
16. Fred (*put*) two or three photographs in his billfold.
17. Fred (*send*) the other photographs to his mother and father.

HEARING AND SPEAKING LESSON 🔊 32

Listen carefully. Answer the questions with a full sentence.

1. The Browns took a trip.
2. They went to South America.
3.
4.
5.
6.
7.
8.
9.
10.
11.

HEARING AND SPEAKING LESSON 🔊 33

Listen carefully. Answer the questions with a full sentence.

1. Fred bought a camera from his Friend Bill last month.
2. His friend Bill sold the camera to him for eighty dollars.
3.
4.
5.
6.
7.
8.
9.
10.
11.
12.
13.
14.
15.
16.
17.

"THE PARTY" 34

Use the past tense form of the verb in parentheses in each sentence.

1. My wife and I (*go*) to the party at Bill's house last night.
2. My wife (*wear*) her new silk dress to the party.
3. The party (*begin*) at eight-thirty, but we (*leave*) at eight.
4. We (*meet*) our friends at their house before the party.
5. We (*drive*) our car to their house.
6. Our friends (*ride*) to the party in our car.
7. Fortunately, I (*know*) almost everyone at the party.
8. My wife and I (*speak*) to most of the guests.
9. Everyone (*eat*) lots of sandwiches and cake at the party.
10. Everyone (*drink*) a lot of coffee and beer at the party.
11. Mr. Brown (*tell*) us all about his trip to South America.
12. Tom and Fred (*bring*) a guitar and an accordion to the party.
13. We (*sing*) all of our favorite songs at the party.
14. Everyone (*have*) a very good time at Bill's party.
15. After the party, my wife and I (*feel*) tired and sleepy.

"MY BAD DAY" 35

Use the past tense form of the verb in parentheses in each sentence.

1. Yesterday (*be*) a very bad day for me.
2. I (*begin*) the day with an accident.
3. I (*cut*) my hand with a razor blade.
4. I (*forget*) about the meeting.
5. Then I (*tear*) my new suit.
6. I (*bet*) on a baseball game next.
7. Unfortunately, I (*lose*) my money.
8. Then a thief (*steal*) my billfold.
9. Fortunately, the police (*catch*) the thief a little while later.
10. Later I (*fall*) on some slippery steps and (*hurt*) my arm.
11. Then a little boy (*throw*) a ball and (*hit*) me accidentally.
12. Next an angry dog (*bite*) me and (*tear*) the seat of my pants.
13. After that, I (*fall down*) again and (*break*) my new watch.
14. As a climax, I (*find*) a ten-dollar parking ticket on my car!

HEARING AND SPEAKING LESSON 34

Listen carefully. Answer the questions with a full sentence.

1. *My wife and I went to the party at Bill's house last night.*
2. *My wife wore her new silk dress to the party.*
3.
4.
5.
6.
7.
8.
9.
10.
11.
12.
13.
14.
15.

HEARING AND SPEAKING LESSON 35

Listen carefully. Answer the questions with a full sentence.

1. *Yesterday was a very bad day for me.*
2. *I began the day with an accident.*
3.
4.
5.
6.
7.
8.
9.
10.
11.
12.
13.
14.

QUESTIONS ABOUT "THE BROWN'S TRIP" 36

Give a complete answer for each of the following questions.

1. Did the Browns take a trip last summer?
2. Did the Browns drive to South America?
3. Did Mr. and Mrs. Brown spend much time in Mexico?
4. Did they have a good time in Bogota, Colombia?
5. Did the Browns write letters to their friends?
6. Did they buy gifts for their friends in all of the countries?

QUESTIONS ABOUT "THE PHOTOGRAPHER" 37

Give a complete answer for each of the following questions.

1. Did Fred buy a camera from his friend Bill?
2. Did Fred pay very much for the camera?
3. Did Fred know a lot about photography at that time?
4. Did Bill give Fred a book with complete instructions?
5. Did Fred take a lot of pictures of his friends?
6. Did Fred put any photographs in his billfold?

QUESTIONS ABOUT "THE PARTY" 38

Give a complete answer for each of the following questions.

1. Did you go to a party at Bill's house last night?
2. Did you meet your friends before the party?
3. Did the party begin at seven-thirty or eight-thirty?
4. Did everyone eat sandwiches and drink coffee at the party?
5. Did everyone have a good time at the party last night?
6. Did Tom and Bill bring musical instruments to the party?
7. Did you feel very tired and sleepy after the party?

QUESTIONS ABOUT "MY BAD DAY" 39

Give a complete answer for each of the following questions.

1. Was yesterday a very bad day for you?
2. Did you cut your hand with a razor blade?
3. Did you forget about that important meeting in the morning?
4. Did you lose all of your money on the baseball game?
5. Did you fall on those slippery steps and hurt your arm?
6. Did a dog bite you and tear the seat of your pants?
7. Did you get a parking ticket from a police officer?

HEARING AND SPEAKING LESSON 36

Listen carefully. Answer the questions with a full sentence.

1 *Yes, the Browns took a trip last summer.*
2
3
4
5
6

HEARING AND SPEAKING LESSON 37

Listen carefully. Answer the questions with a full sentence.

1 *Yes, Fred bought a camera from his friend Bill.*
2
3
4
5
6

HEARING AND SPEAKING LESSON 38

Listen carefully. Answer the questions with a full sentence.

1 *Yes, we went to the party at Bill's house last night.*
2
3
4
5
6
7

HEARING AND SPEAKING LESSON 39

Listen carefully. Answer the questions with a full sentence.

1 *Yes, yesterday was a very bad day for me.*
2
3
4
5
6
7

FREE WRITING PRACTICE(2)

What's this?
this is a man.
this is a man.

Is this a woman?
no, this is not a woman.
no, this is not a woman.

What's this?
this is a woman.
this is a woman.

Is this a man?
no, this is not a man.
no, this is not a man.

Are you a woman(man)?
yes, I am a woman.
yes, I am a man.

FREE WRITING PRACTICE(3) 🔊

What can you see?

I can see a table.

I can see a table.

I can see a chair.

I can see a chair.

I can see a book.

I can see a book.

I can see a table, a chair and a book.

IRREGULAR VERB QUIZ(1)   40

Select the correct verb for each sentence. Use each verb only once. Use only the past tense form of the verb.

choose
feel
take
send
go √
meet
lose
stand
fall
blow
grow
break
hurt
hear

1. The boys <u>went</u> home an hour ago.
2. That tree ---- three feet last year.
3. Bill ---- a pretty tie from the rack.
4. I ---- a course in American history.
5. The little boy ---- the glass window.
6. Alice ---- her pen at school yesterday.
7. Mother ---- very sick this morning.
8. They ---- a letter to Mr. Walter yesterday.
9. We ---- his speech on the radio.
10. The wind ---- very hard last night.
11. I ---- on the corner for half an hour.
12. We ---- our friends there at 5:00 p.m.
13. He ---- on the ice and ---- his arm.

IRREGULAR VERB QUIZ(2)   41

Select the correct verb for each sentence. Use each verb only once. Use only the past tense form of the verb.

build
put
fall
feel
fly
bite
steal
tear
cut
begin √
write
drive
lend
shut
wear

1. Last year, this class <u>began</u> at 8:30 p.m.
2. Mary ---- on the slippery steps today.
3. The Browns ---- a new house last year.
4. The thief ---- jewelry from that store.
5. Miss Davis ---- to Cuba with her sister.
6. Frank ---- us a long letter last week.
7. He ---- his hand with a sharp knife.
8. Mary ---- her new dress to the party.
9. Bill ---- me fifteen dollars yesterday.
10. The man ---- the door very quietly.
11. Mr. Wilson ---- the car carefully.
12. She ---- the dictionary beside the typewriter.
13. We ---- happy because of the news.
14. The dog ---- me and ---- my clothes.

HEARING AND SPEAKING LESSON 40

Listen carefully. Answer the questions with a full sentence.

1. *The boys went home an hour ago.*
2. *The tree grew three feet last year.*
3.
4.
5.
6.
7.
8.
9.
10.
11.
12.
13.

HEARING AND SPEAKING LESSON 41

Listen carefully. Answer the questions with a full sentence.

1. *Last year, this class began at 8:30 p.m.*
2. *Mary fell on the slippery steps today.*
3.
4.
5.
6.
7.
8.
9.
10.
11.
12.
13.
14.

IRREGULAR VERB QUIZ(3)   42

Select the correct verb for each sentence. Use each verb only once. Use only the past tense form of the verb.

sleep	1	John ---- the answers to the questions.
find	2	I ---- the back door a few minutes ago.
speak	3	He ---- for ten hours last night.
drive	4	Bill ---- to the teacher about that.
know	5	I ---- to work by bus this morning.
bring	6	Fred ---- quite sick last night.
tell	7	Betty ---- the dishes on the shelf.
shut	8	Mr. Harris ---- that class last year.
ride	9	We ---- ten dollars over the weekend.
spend	10	Charles ---- a friend to the party.
feel	11	The teacher ---- the students the answer.
put	12	Frank ---- the car very carefully.
teach	13	I ---- the answer in the appendix.

IRREGULAR VERB QUIZ(4)   43

Select the correct verb for each sentence. Use each verb only once. Use only the past tense form of the verb.

teach	1	The men ---- for Chicago last Tuesday.
win	2	Frank ---- to school with his friend.
ride	3	Professor Moore ---- American history last year.
tear	4	They ---- the news from their friend.
begin	5	The students ---- the story carefully.
leave	6	Our car ---- the other car very hard.
hear	7	Fred ---- his old car to Mr. Brown.
pay	8	She ---- her bracelet under a chair.
find	9	Fred ---- the camera from Bill.
speak	10	Fred ---- for the camera in cash.
buy	11	He ---- to his boss about that matter.
hit	12	The meeting ---- at eight-thirty.
sell	13	She ---- the paper into two pieces.
read	14	Miss Davis ---- a prize in that contest.

HEARING AND SPEAKING LESSON 42

Listen carefully. Answer the questions with a full sentence.

1. *John knew the answer to the question.*
2. *I shut the back door a few minutes ago.*
3.
4.
5.
6.
7.
8.
9.
10.
11.
12.
13.

HEARING AND SPEAKING LESSON 43

Listen carefully. Answer the questions with a full sentence.

1. *The men left for Chicago last Tuesday.*
2. *Frank rode to school with with hi friend.*
3.
4.
5.
6.
7.
8.
9.
10.
11.
12.
13.
14.

IRREGULAR VERB QUIZ(5)

Select the correct verb for each sentence. Use each verb only once. Use only the past tense form of the verb.

bring 1 Our team ---- the baseball game yesterday.
cut 2 Mr. Smith ---- his job last Thursday.
break 3 The other suit ---- me very well.
catch 4 The man ---- the rope with a knife.
throw 5 The boy ---- the butter on his bread.
drive 6 My brother ---- me twenty-five dollars.
fit 7 The boys ---- the window with a ball.
win 8 He ---- the ball to me, and I ---- it.
buy 9 The teacher ---- in front of the blackboard.
quit 10 Fred's new camera ---- eighty dollars.
spread 11 The Browns ---- a new house last month.
cost 12 We ---- to Cincinnati in five hours.
stand 13 The students ---- their dictionaries to class.
lend

IRREGULAR VERB QUIZ(6)

Select the correct verb for each sentence. Use each verb only once. Use only the past tense form of the verb.

stand 1 He ---- the name of the book.
throw 2 She ---- the paper into the wastebasket.
sit 3 The meeting ---- at eight o'clock sharp.
make 4 He ---- the money under the books.
cut 5 I ---- in the seat right behind Frank.
hold 6 You ---- some mistakes on the test.
cost 7 They ---- us fifteen dollars yesterday.
fit 8 We ---- on the corner for half an hour.
begin 9 The boys ---- the big box very carefully.
forget 10 His new suit ---- eighty-five dollars.
keep 11 Tom and Ed ---- dinner with Mr. Harris.
lend 12 Fred ---- his hand with a sharp knife.
have 13 We ---- our car in a garage last winter.
hide 14 Edward's new suit ---- him very well.

HEARING AND SPEAKING LESSON 🔊   **44**

Listen carefully. Answer the questions with a full sentence.

1. *Our team won the baseball game yesterday.*
2. *Mr. Smith quit his job last Thursday.*
3.
4.
5.
6.
7.
8.
9.
10.
11.
12.
13.

HEARING AND SPEAKING LESSON 🔊   **45**

Listen carefully. Answer the questions with a full sentence.

1. *He forgot the name of the book.*
2. *She threw the paper into the wastebasket.*
3.
4.
5.
6.
7.
8.
9.
10.
11.
12.
13.
14.

REVIEW : QUESTIONS WITH BE   46

Change the following statements to questions. Study the first three examples carefully.

1. The men are here now. —*Are the men here now?*
2. The men are working now. —*Are the men working now?*
3. There are students in the room. —*Are there students in the room?*
4. Frank is taking a course in German this semester.
5. The house right next to theirs is Mr. Johnson's.
6. The last lesson was difficult for the students.
7. Miss Peters is writing letters for Mr. Johnson right now.
8. There were a lot of people at Bill's party last night.
9. The men were very tired after all of that hard work.
10. Smith and Green are collecting information for Mr. Johnson.
11. There are many clerks in that big department store.
12. It is raining very hard right now.
13. The man in front of Frank is Mr. Anderson.
14. Mr. Brown is reading the evening newspaper right now.

REVIEW : QUESTIONS WITH DO   47

Change the following statements to questions. Study the first three examples carefully.

1. The man drives very fast. —*Does the man drive very fast?*
2. The man worked very hard. —*Did the man work very hard?*
3. The man spoke very fast. —*Did the man speak very fast?*
4. Mr. Wilson flies to Los Angeles once a month.
5. Those two women come from South America.
6. The secretary understood Mr. Wilson's instructions completely.
7. Mr. and Mrs. Johnson borrowed the money from a bank.
8. They watch television every night of the week.
9. Mr. Moore teaches English from nine o'clock to eleven o'clock.
10. Miss Graniero always does her homework very carefully.
11. Tom's friend put his hat and overcoat in the closet.
12. Mr. Johnson works thirty-five hours a week.
13. Miss Peters wrote all of the reports for Mr. Johnson.
14. The two mechanics did that work very quickly.

HEARING AND SPEAKING LESSON 46

Listen carefully. Answer the questions with a full sentence.

1. *Are there men here now?*
2. *Are the men working now?*
3.
4.
5.
6.
7.
8.
9.
10.
11.
12.
13.
14.

HEARING AND SPEAKING LESSON 47

Listen carefully. Answer the questions with a full sentence.

1. *Does the man drive very fast?*
2. *Did the man work very hard?*
3.
4.
5.
6.
7.
8.
9.
10.
11.
12.
13.
14.

THE FUTURE TENSE WITH WILL 48

Use the future tense of the verb in parentheses in each sentence. Use only the future tense with *will*. Study the first three examples carefully.

1. He (*leave*) early tomorrow. —*He will leave early tomorrow.*
2. We (*see*) him next week. —*We will see him next week.*
3. They (*be*) here in ten minutes. —*They will be here in ten minutes.*
4. The meeting (*begin*) at nine o'clock tonight.
5. I (*give*) Mr. Brown your message tomorrow night.
6. Mr. Moore (*read*) that story to the students next Monday.
7. The janitor (*lock*) the door to the office at 6:30 p.m.
8. We (*have*) an important holiday two months from now.
9. The men (*be*) here at one-thirty this afternoon.
10. I (*remind*) Mr. Wilson of his appointment with you tonight.
11. Mr. Johnson's wife (*buy*) refreshments for the party.
12. All of the people (*be*) ready at ten o'clock tomorrow morning.
13. Mr. Pennyweight (*return*) to England a week from tomorrow.
14. Our friends (*meet*) us at the subway station at five o'clock.

USING THE FUTURE TENSE(1) 49

Change the verb in each sentence to the future tense with *will*. If necessary, change the expression of time(change *yesterday* to *tomorrow, etc.*).

1. We ate lunch with John. —*We will eat lunch with John.*
2. I returned and asked him. —*I will return and ask him.*
3. John spoke to the director's secretary about that matter.
4. Charles went to the movies with his friends last night.
5. The Wilsons flew to Brazil and Argentina last year.
6. The clerk wrapped the package and gave her the change.
7. Our guests saw almost all of the city during their vacation.
8. The student wrote a description of his city for the teacher.
9. My friend Edward lent me the money a week ago.
10. Bill sold his camera to Fred and bought a new one.
11. They read that historical novel three weeks ago.
12. Mr. Johnson wore his new winter overcoat to work.
13. My secretary got to the office on time this morning.
14. We got up early and had our breakfast at 7:30.

HEARING AND SPEAKING LESSON 48

Listen carefully. Answer the questions with a full sentence.

1. *He will leave early tomorrow.*
2. *We will see him next week.*
3.
4.
5.
6.
7.
8.
9.
10.
11.
12.
13.
14.

HEARING AND SPEAKING LESSON 49

Listen carefully. Answer the questions with a full sentence.

1. *We will eat lunch with John.*
2. *I will return and ask him.*
3.
4.
5.
6.
7.
8.
9.
10.
11.
12.
13.
14.

THE FUTURE TENSE WITH GO — 50

Use the future tense of the verb in parentheses in each sentence. Use only the future tense with *go*. Study the first four examples carefully.

1. I (*finish*) it next week. —*I am going to finish it next week.*
2. He (*go*) there tomorrow. —*He is going to go there tomorrow.*
3. We (*be*) at the meeting. —*We are going to be at the meeting.*
4. I (*return*) and (*ask*) him. —*I am going to return and ask him.*
5. The teacher (*explain*) the next lesson to us tomorrow.
6. We (*attend*) that conference in St. Louis next month.
7. I (*study*) my English lesson with my friends tonight.
8. Mr. Wilson and Mr. Johnson (*be*) in the office all afternoon.
9. We (*go*) to the movies with our friends tomorrow night.
10. Miss Anderson (*invite*) all of her friends to her party.
11. Mr. Harris (*teach*) a different English class next year.
12. My brother (*go*) to Baltimore with me next week.
13. The men (*repair*) the roof of the house the day after tomorrow.
14. There (*be*) an important meeting here next Thursday evening.

USING THE FUTURE TENSE (2) — 51

Change the verb in each sentence to the future tense with *go*. If necessary, change the expression of time (change *yesterday* to *tomorrow*, etc.).

1. We went there last night. —*We are going to go there tomorrow night.*
2. I saw him two days ago. —*I am going to see him two days from now.*
3. The students read the assignment carefully yesterday.
4. John spoke to Professor Taylor about that last Thursday.
5. Mr. and Mrs. Brown bought a new house last year.
6. Mr. Foster quit his job with the Ajax Company.
7. I sent my friend a letter and told him about everything.
8. Mr. Moore was the teacher of this class last year.
9. She picked up the paper and threw it into the wastebasket.
10. Tom and Bill had dinner with Mr. Moore and Mr. Harris.
11. Mrs. Johnson wore her new spring coat to the party yesterday.
12. The president made an important announcement over the radio.
13. My wife bought a new winter overcoat this week.
14. The Browns sold their old house last year and bought a new one.

HEARING AND SPEAKING LESSON 50

Listen carefully. Answer the questions with a full sentence.

1. *I am going to finish it next week.*
2. *He is going to go there tomorrow.*
3.
4.
5.
6.
7.
8.
9.
10.
11.
12.
13.
14.

HEARING AND SPEAKING LESSON 51

Listen carefully. Answer the questions with a full sentence.

1. *We are going to go there tomorrow night.*
2. *I am going to see him two days from now.*
3.
4.
5.
6.
7.
8.
9.
10.
11.
12.
13.
14.

QUESTIONS : THE FUTURE WITH WILL   52

Change the following statements to questions. Notice the examples.

1. He will go by train. —*Will he go by train?*
2. They will be there. —*Will they be there?*
3. Mr. and Mrs. Wilson will arrive in Detroit on Monday.
4. You will finish all of the work before tomorrow.
5. Many people will attend the meeting tomorrow night.
6. There will be enough food and coffee for everyone.
7. All of the students will copy the list of words from the book.
8. Mr. and Mrs. Anderson will be in Madison a week from now.
9. Your friends will help you with your homework tonight.
10. Mr. Johnson will mail that important letter tomorrow.
11. Dinner will be ready at 7:00 p.m. tonight.
12. The messenger will deliver the package to your house.
13. There will be an important announcement over the radio tonight.
14. Mr. and Mrs. Anderson will return from New York by train.

QUESTIONS : THE FUTURE WITH GO   53

Change the following statements to questions. Notice the examples.

1. He is going to leave early. —*Is he going to leave early?*
2. They are going to be there. —*Are they going to be there?*
3. Bill Brown is going to eat lunch with us today.
4. Mr. Foster is going to quit his job with the Ajax Company.
5. All of the students are going to go to the lecture tonight.
6. You are going to accept his offer for a job with that company.
7. There is going to be a party here next Friday night.
8. His friends are going to leave here the day after tomorrow.
9. Professor Moore is going to explain that lesson to them.
10. We are going to watch that television program tonight.
11. Both Fred and Tom are going to be at the meeting tomorrow.
12. Mrs. Johnson is going to wear her new dress this evening.
13. Mr. Brown is going to take his vacation in August.
14. Frank's friends are going to go to the movies with us tonight.

HEARING AND SPEAKING LESSON 52

Listen carefully. Answer the questions with a full sentence.

1. *Will he go by train?*
2. *Will they be there?*
3.
4.
5.
6.
7.
8.
9.
10.
11.
12.
13.
14.

HEARING AND SPEAKING LESSON 53

Listen carefully. Answer the questions with a full sentence.

1. *Is he going to leave early?*
2. *Are they going to be there?*
3.
4.
5.
6.
7.
8.
9.
10.
11.
12.
13.
14.

NEGATIVES : THE FUTURE WITH WILL   54

Change the following statements to negatives. Study the examples.

1. He will explain that lesson. —*He won't explain that lesson.*
2. We will be at the meeting. —*We won't be at the meeting.*
3. Our friends will go to that part of the city tomorrow.
4. The Andersons will leave California before January tenth.
5. Mr. Johnson's secretary will be in the office today.
6. Mr. Berg will attend his English class tonight.
7. There will be a meeting here next Thursday evening.
8. The Andersons will stop in Denver on their way to New York.
9. Miss Peters will finish those reports before Wednesday.
10. Frank and I will be at the library this afternoon.
11. Uncle Dan will eat dinner with us next Sunday.
12. We will need your help with that work tomorrow.
13. The students will be ready for the examination next week.
14. Wilson will read Mr. Johnson's reports this afternoon.

NEGATIVES : THE FUTURE WITH GO   55

Change the following statements to negatives. Study the examples.

1. They are going to return. —*They aren't going to return.*
2. She is going to be there. —*She isn't going to be there.*
3. The Browns are going to buy a new house this year.
4. I am going to answer John's letter this evening.
5. My friend Frank is going to join that club.
6. Miss Stewart and I are going to go shopping this afternoon.
7. The Johnsons' friends are going to be at the party.
8. I am going to ask Mr. Wilson for his advice in this matter.
9. The workers in that company are going to join a union.
10. Pierre is going to work for a degree at the university.
11. The boss is going to hire another assistant.
12. There are going to be many people here tomorrow night.
13. Smith is going to accept Mr. Wilson's offer for a job.
14. We are going to listen to that radio program this evening.

HEARING AND SPEAKING LESSON 54

Listen carefully. Answer the questions with a full sentence.

1. *He won't explain that lesson.*
2. *We won't be at the meeting.*
3.
4.
5.
6.
7.
8.
9.
10.
11.
12.
13.
14.

HEARING AND SPEAKING LESSON 55

Listen carefully. Answer the questions with a full sentence.

1. *They aren't going to return.*
2. *She isn't going to be there.*
3.
4.
5.
6.
7.
8.
9.
10.
11.
12.
13.
14.

USING THE FUTURE TENSES (3)   56

Use the future with go in place of the future with *will*.

1. I will leave very soon. —*I am going to leave very soon.*
2. He will be ready at five. —*He is going to be ready at five.*
3. I will mail the letter to my brother this afternoon.
4. The president will make an important speech tomorrow.
5. There will be a concert in the park on Friday night.
6. We will eat dinner at six or six-thirty tonight.
7. Mr. Smith will meet us right here after the meeting.
8. Will you be at the library until four o'clock?
9. She won't clean the house until next Monday morning.
10. Our guests will leave for Wisconsin tomorrow night.
11. Will you stop in Miami on your way to South America?
12. Will Mr. Wilson and Mrs. Johnson be in the office tomorrow?
13. There won't be many people in the office this afternoon.
14. The plumber will fix the leak in the bathroom tomorrow.

USING THE FUTURE TENSES (4)   57

Use the future with will in place of the future with *go*.

1. We are going to go tonight. —*We will go tonight.*
2. She is going to be there too. —*She will be there too.*
3. Our teacher is going to help us with that lesson.
4. Miss Graniero is going to meet us after class today.
5. Are you going to accept Mr. Wilson's offer for a job?
6. I'm going to study my assignment with Fred tonight.
7. His friend isn't going to leave until next Thursday or Friday.
8. There's going to be an important meeting here tomorrow.
9. Are you going to be in your office tomorrow afternoon?
10. No, I'm not going to be in my office tomorrow afternoon.
11. Is Mr. Wilson going to hire a new secretary next week?
12. Mr. Johnson is going to ride to work with Mr. Smith today.
13. We aren't going to go to Miami by train this time.
14. I'm going to return all of the books to you tomorrow morning.

HEARING AND SPEAKING LESSON 56

Listen carefully. Answer the questions with a full sentence.

1. *I am going to leave very soon.*
2. *He is going to be ready at five.*
3.
4.
5.
6.
7.
8.
9.
10.
11.
12.
13.
14.

HEARING AND SPEAKING LESSON 57

Listen carefully. Answer the questions with a full sentence.

1. *We will go tonight.*
2. *She will be there too.*
3.
4.
5.
6.
7.
8.
9.
10.
11.
12.
13.
14.

FREE WRITING PRACTICE(4) 🔊

What's this?
this is a boy.

What is he doing?
he is running.

What is he doing?
he is sitting on the chair.

What is he doing?
he is pushing the chair.

What is he doing?
he is pulling the table.

FREE WRITING PRACTICE(5) 🔊

This is a box.

this is a box.

this is a box.

pen

ink

paper

pencil

scissors

ruler

What can you see in the box?

I can see a pen in the box.
I can see a pencil in the box.
I can see a paper in the box.
I can see ink in the box.
I can see a ruler in the box.
I can see scissors in the box.

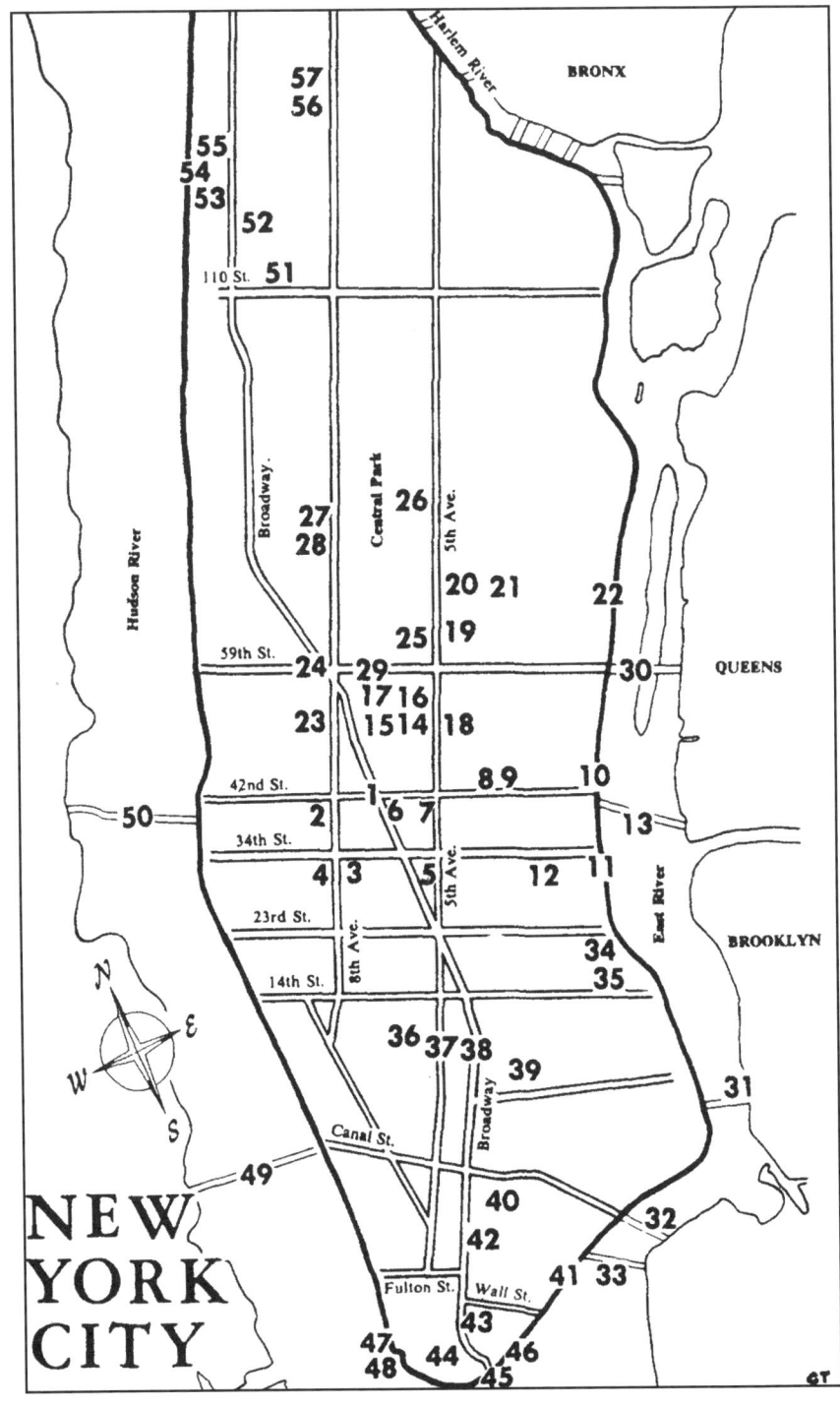

WELCOME TO NEW YORK

Manhattan, New York

GUIDE TO MAP : **1** Times Square. **2** the Port Authority Bus Terminal. **3** Pennsylvania Station. **4** the U.S. General Post Office. **5** the Empire State Building. **6** the Metropolitan Opera House. **7** the New York Public Library. **8** Grand Central Station. **9** the Chrysler Building. **10** the United Nations. **11** the New York University-Bellevue Medical Center. **12** the East Side Airlines Terminal. **13** the Queens Midtown Tunnel. **14** Rockefeller Center. **15** Radio City Music Hall. **16** the Museum of Modern Art. **17** the Whitney Museum. **18** St. Patrick's Cathedral. **19** Temple Emanu-El. **20** the Frick Museum. **21** Hunter College. **22** New York Hospital of Cornell Medical Center. **23** Madison Square Garden. **24** the New York Coliseum. **25** the Central Park Zoo. **26** the Metropolitan Museum of Art. **27** the Hayden Planetarium. **28** the Museum of Natural History. **29** Carnegie Hall. **30** the Queensboro Bridge. **31** the Williamsburg Bridge. **32** the Manhattan Bridge. **33** the Brooklyn Bridge. **34** Peter Cooper Village. **35** Stuyvesant Town. **36** Greenwich Village. **37** Washington Square. **38** New York University (downtown section). **39** the Bowery. **40** Chinatown. **41** the Fulton Fish Market **42** City Hall. **43** the New York Stock Exchange. **44** Battery Park. **45** the Battery Tunnel to Brooklyn. **46** the Ferry to Staten Island. **47** the Ferry to Ellis Island. **48** the Ferry to the Statue of Liberty. **49** the Holland Tunnel. **50**. the Lincoln Tunnel. **51** Cathedral of St. John the Divine. **52** Columbia University. **53** Riverside Church. **54** Grant's Tomb. **55** the International House. **56** City College of New York (C.C.N.Y.). **57** Lewisohn Stadium.

"A TRIP TO NEW YORK"

Central Park, New York

Mr. and Mrs. Anderson *are going to take* a trip from California to New York. They *will leave* California on Sunday. They *are going to go* by air. They *will arrive* at the airport at 2:00 Sunday afternoon. The plane *will leave* for New York at 2:30. Therefore, they *will arrive* in New York that night. They *are going to stay* at a hotel near Times Square.

They *will get up* early on Monday. They *will eat* breakfast and *leave* the hotel before nine o'clock. They *are going to walk* through the area between 34th Street and 42nd Street. They *will start* at Pennsylvania Station at 34th Street. Then they *will go* to Macy's and Gimbel's, two of New York's largest department stores, on Sixth Avenue. They *will* also *visit* the Empire State Building(1472ft.). They *are going to go* up to the top of the building. They *will see* all of New York City from there. Then they *are going to walk* to the Metropolitan Opera house and the famous New York Public Library. They *are going to go* to bed early that night. They *will be* very tired.

They *are going to walk* to First Avenue and 42nd Street on Tuesday. But on the way, they're *going to stop* at Grand Central Station. Then they *will go* to the beautiful United Nations buildings along the East River. They *will go* on a guided tour through the buildings. Next they *will walk* down the street to the New York University-Bellevue Medical Center between 34th Street and 30th Street. Then they *will return* to their hotel. They're *going to eat* dinner with some old friends that evening.

They *are going to walk* along Park Avenue and Fifth Avenue on Wednesday. Mrs. Anderson *is going to buy* presents for her relatives in some of the Fifth Avenue stores.

After that, they *will go* west to the theater district between 40th Street and 46th Street. They *are going to attend* a popular Broadway play that evening.

Mr. and Mrs. Anderson *will see* the area north of 46th Street on Thursday. They *will spend* several hours at Rockefeller Center. They *will see* the Radio City Music Hall there too. In this same general area, they *will* also *visit* the Museum of Modern Art, the Whitney Museum, the Temple Emanu-El, St. Patrick's Cathedral, and Hunter College. Finally, they *will go* crosstown to Madison Square Garden and the New York Coliseum at Columbus Circle.

They *are going to visit* the zoo in Central Park on Friday. Their other stops on that day *will be* at the Metropolitan Museum of Art, the Museum of Natural History, and the Hayden Planetarium. They *are going to attend* a concert at Carnegie Hall that evening.

They *are going to drive* through downtown New York on Saturday. They *will see* several large bridges along the East River. They *will go* through Greenwich Village. At nearby Washington Square, they *are going to visit* the downtown section of New York University, one of the largest universities in the world. After that, they *will visit* the Bowery, Chinatown, City Hall, Wall Street and Battery Park. They *will finish* their day with a trip to the Statue of Liberty on Bedloe Island by ferry boat.

The Andersons *are going to visit* Columbia University at 116th Street and Broadway on Sunday. They *will* also *see* the Cathedral of St. John the Divine, the Riverside Church, Grant's Tomb, and the International House all in the same general area. They *will meet* students and visitors from all over the world at the International House. Later in the day, they *are going to drive* to C.C.N.Y., Lewisohn Stadium, the Polo Grounds, Yankee Stadium, and the Cloisters at 198th Street. They *will end* their day at the world famous Bronx Zoo.

Mr. and Mrs. Anderson *are going to return* to California by train. In this way, they *will see* much more of the country. They *will get back* to Los Angeles on Wednesday. Of course, *they are going to describe* their wonderful trip to all of their friends.

QUESTIONS ABOUT "A TRIP TO NEW YORK"

Give a complete answer for each of the following questions.

1. Are Mr. and Mrs. Anderson going to take a trip?
2. Will they leave California on Saturday or Sunday?
3. Are they going to go to New York by train or by air?
4. Will the plane leave for New York at 2:00 or 2:30?
5. Are they going to stay at a hotel on Park Avenue?
6. Are they going to eat breakfast and leave the hotel early?
7. Will they have much trouble with directions in New York?
8. Are they going to see the Empire State Building?
9. Will they go to the zoo in Central Park on Monday?
10. Are they going to visit the New York Public Library?
11. Will they be very tired at the end of their first day?
12. Are they going to go to bed very late on Monday night?
13. Will they go through the United Nations Buildings?
14. Are the Andersons going to go to their hotel after that?
15. Are they going to eat dinner with friends on Tuesday night?
16. Will they stay at their hotel on the following day?
17. Are they going to go to the downtown section on Wednesday?
18. Are they going to walk along Park Avenue and Fifth Avenue on Wednesday?
19. Is Mrs. Anderson going to buy presents for her relatives?
20. Will the Andersons attend a Broadway play that night?
21. Are they going to spend time at Rockefeller Center too?
22. Will they visit any museums in this same area?
23. Are they going to visit the zoo in Central Park on Friday?
24. Are they going to drive through downtown New York?
25. Will they see Columbia University or New York University?
26. Are they going to drive through Greenwich Village too?
27. Will the Andersons return to California on Saturday?
28. Are they going to see the downtown section on Sunday?
29. Are the Andersons going to visit the International House?
30. Will the Andersons describe their trip to all of their friends?
31. Are they going to return to California by plane?
32. Will they get back to Los Angeles on Wednesday?
33. Are the Andersons going to go to New York next year?

HEARING AND SPEAKING LESSON 🔊

Listen carefully. Answer the questions with a full sentence.

1. *Yes, the Andersons are going to take a trip from California to New York.*
2. *They will leave California on Sunday.*
3.
4.
5.
6.
7.
8.
9.
10.
11.
12.
13.
14.
15.
16.
17.
18.
19.
20.
21.
22.
23.
24.
25.
26.
27.
28.
29.
30.
31.
32.
33.

MUCH, MANY, AND VERY (1)

Use *much*, *many*, or *very* in the blank space or spaces in each sentence.

1. We made ---- sandwiches.
2. Did you buy ---- meat?
3. The food was ---- delicious.
4. We bought ---- food for the party.
5. The guests drank ---- coffee.
6. Was the coffee ---- strong?
7. I enjoy coffee ---- ----.
8. I don't drink ---- ---- milk.
9. You didn't invite ---- ---- guests.
10. There were ---- glasses on the table in the dining room.
11. There was ---- milk and coffee in the kitchen.
12. There weren't ---- ---- people at the party last night.
13. Mary and Louise bought ---- bread for the sandwiches.
14. The two girls used ---- pieces of bread for the sandwiches.

MUCH, MANY, AND VERY (2)

Use *much*, *many*, or *very* in the blank space or spaces in each sentence.

1. Our last two English lessons were ---- long.
2. The students had ---- difficulty with the last lesson.
3. Did you have ---- trouble with the homework today?
4. The last lesson was ---- difficult for everyone.
5. Did you spend ---- time on your homework last night?
6. I wrote each new word in the lesson ---- times.
7. Does your English teacher give you ---- homework?
8. Mr. Harris, our teacher, has a ---- clear voice.
9. Our teacher speaks ---- slowly and ---- clearly.
10. We learn ---- new English words in class every day.
11. Does your friend Roger speak ---- ---- English?
12. Do Mr. Meyer and Mr. Berg speak English ---- well?
13. On the whole, the English language is ---- easy.
14. ---- people all over the world speak English these days.

HEARING AND SPEAKING LESSON 60

Listen carefully. Answer the questions with a full sentence.

1. *We made many sandwiches.*
2. *Did you buy much meat?*
3. *The food was very delicious.*
4.
5.
6.
7.
8.
9.
10.
11.
12.
13.
14.

HEARING AND SPEAKING LESSON 61

Listen carefully. Answer the questions with a full sentence.

1. *Our last two English lesson were very long.*
2. *The students had much difficulty with the last lesson.*
3.
4.
5.
6.
7.
8.
9.
10.
11.
12.
13.
14.

A LOT OF AND LOTS OF   62

Substitute the expressions *a lot of* and *lots of* for *much* or *many* in each sentence.

1. John spends *much* time on his assignments.
   —John spends *a lot of* time on his assignments.
   —John spends *lots of* time on his assignments.
2. There are *many* people in the auditorium now.
   —There are *a lot of* people in the auditorium now.
   —There are *lots of* people in the auditorium now.
3. The students learn many new words every day.
4. Mr. Burlington drinks much coffee every day.
5. There are many short words in the English language.
6. Miss Cunningham puts much cream in her coffee.
7. That student from Japan has many friends in this class.
8. Frank receives many letters from his friends and relatives.
9. There are many students in the classroom right now.
10. We had much trouble with the sentences on that page.

TOO, TOO MUCH, AND TOO MANY   63

Use *too*, *too much*, or *too many* in the blank space in each sentence.

1. The waitress put ---- cream and sugar in my coffee.
2. You made ---- mistakes. Write the lesson again.
3. Mr. Duncan gave us ---- homework. It was ---- difficult.
4. There are ---- people in this room. It's ---- hot!
5. You spoke ---- fast and used ---- hard words for me.
6. There are ---- pictures and ---- different colors in this room.
7. The radio is ---- loud now. It's making ---- noise.
8. I drank ---- coffee and ate ---- sandwiches last night.
9. There are ---- things in the suitcase. It's ---- heavy.
10. You put ----- water in the glasses. They're ---- full.
11. That old house is ---- large and has ---- rooms.
12. That program has ---- advertising and ---- interruptions.
13. That work took ---- time. It was ---- trouble for us.
14. That fellow was ---- impatient. He made mistakes ---- times.

HEARING AND SPEAKING LESSON 62

Listen carefully. Answer the questions with a full sentence.

1. *John spends a lot of time on his assignments.*
2. *John spends lots of time on his assignments.*
3.
4.
5.
6.
7.
8.
9.
10.

HEARING AND SPEAKING LESSON 63

Listen carefully. Answer the questions with a full sentence.

1. *The waitress put too much cream and sugar in my coffee.*
2. *You made too many mistakes. Write the lesson again.*
3.
4.
5.
6.
7.
8.
9.
10.
11.
12.
13.
14.

THE WORDS SOME AND ANY 64

Use *some* or *any* in the blank space in each sentence. Study the examples.

1. There are *some* students in the room now.
2. Are there *any* students in the classroom now?
3. I had *some* trouble with my homework last night.
4. I didn't have *any* trouble with my homework last night.
5. There were ---- beautiful pictures on the wall.
6. The students didn't have ---- difficulty with the lesson.
7. The children are eating ---- icecream in the kitchen.
8. Martha doesn't want ---- dessert after dinner tonight.
9. Are there ---- cigarettes in the box on the table?
10. Mr. Duncan didn't give us ---- specific instructions.
11. Are there ---- extra chairs in the other classroom?
12. Your secretary has ---- important messages for you.
13. I'm sorry. I don't have ---- information about that.
14. Did the teacher make ---- comments on your paper?

SOMETHING vs ANYTHING 65

Use *something* or *anything* in the blank space in each sentence.

1. Is there ---- on Mr. Crowell's desk right now?
2. Yes, Mr. Crowell put ---- there a few minutes ago.
3. Did you say ---- to Mr. Lewis about our plans?
4. No, I didn't say ---- at all to him about our plans.
5. Is there ---- in the middle drawer of that desk?
6. There isn't ---- there. I looked in the drawer.
7. Did Mrs. Benson find ---- in the boxes in the closet?
8. Yes, she did. She found ---- in the small red box.
9. Is Mr. Evans going to tell us ---- about his trip?
10. Yes, he's going to tell us ---- about his trip.
11. Did the girls buy ---- at that department store?
12. No, Alice and Louise didn't buy ---- at the store today.
13. Did the mailman bring ---- for me this morning?
14. Yes, he did. There's ---- for you on the desk in your room.

HEARING AND SPEAKING LESSON 64

Listen carefully. Answer the questions with a full sentence.

1. *There are some students in the room now.*
2. *Are there any students in the classroom now?*
3.
4.
5.
6.
7.
8.
9.
10.
11.
12.
13.
14.

HEARING AND SPEAKING LESSON 65

Listen carefully. Answer the questions with a full sentence.

1. *Is there anything on Mr. Crowell's desk right now?*
2. *Yes, Mr. Crowell put something there a few minutes ago.*
3.
4.
5.
6.
7.
8.
9.
10.
11.
12.
13.
14.

SOMEONE vs ANYONE   66

Choose *someone* or *anyone* for the blank space in each sentence.

1. Listen! There is ---- at the front door now.
2. Mr. Benson didn't tell ---- about his suggestion.
3. Did you see ---- in the hall outside my office?
4. Frank doesn't have a book. He lent his to ----.
5. There will be ---- in this office before 9:00 a.m.
6. Please don't tell ---- about this matter until later.
7. Did you ask ---- to help you with the work tomorrow?
8. ---- left this package on your desk this morning.
9. Please give this envelope to ---- in Dean Brown's office.
10. Do you know ---- in the advanced class?
11. There wasn't ---- in the office after 5:30 p.m.
12. ---- told Mr. Duncan the news a few minutes ago.
13. Mr. Meyer didn't talk to ---- about his problem.
14. The secretary is speaking to ---- on the telephone now.

ANYONE vs NO ONE   67

Choose *anyone* or *no one* for the blank space in each sentence.

1. There was ---- at the information desk this morning.
2. There isn't ---- in Mr. Brown's office right now.
3. ---- finished the examination before three o'clock.
4. John didn't see ---- in Dean Brown's office.
5. John saw ---- in the hall outside the office either.
6. He didn't notice ---- in the other room. He's sure of that.
7. ---- in the whole class knew that word.
8. Please don't tell ---- about this until next Friday.
9. I will tell ---- about your plans until that time.
10. ---- knows a thing about this except you and me.
11. I don't know ---- in the other two English classes.
12. I saw ---- from our class at the meeting yesterday.
13. ---- said anything to me about it at the meeting.
14. The chairman didn't get suggestions from ---- in the audience.

HEARING AND SPEAKING LESSON 66

Listen carefully. Answer the questions with a full sentence.

1. *Listen! There is someone at the front door now.*
2. *Mr. Benson didn't tell anyone about this suggestion.*
3.
4.
5.
6.
7.
8.
9.
10.
11.
12.
13.
14.

HEARING AND SPEAKING LESSON 67

Listen carefully. Answer the questions with a full sentence.

1. *There was no one at the information desk this morning.*
2. *There isn't anyone in Mr. Brown's office right now.*
3.
4.
5.
6.
7.
8.
9.
10.
11.
12.
13.
14.

FREE WRITING PRACTICE(6)

What can you see in this picture?

I can see a teacher.
I can see a clock.
I can see students.
I can see desks.
I can see a window.
I can see a door.
I can see a blackboard.
I can see books.

FREE WRITING PRACTICE(7) 🔊

Where are the students?

they are in the classroom.

How many students are there in the classroom?

there are three students in the classroom.

What are they doing in the classroom?

they are studying in the classroom.

What is the teacher doing in the classroom?

she is writing on the blackboard.

Where is the clock?

the clock is on the wall.

Where is the books?

the books are on the desk.

What time is it?

it is ten five a.m.

DIRECT AND INDIRECT OBJECTS   68

PART ONE : THE INDIRECT OBJECT WITH TO

Change the position of the word or words in italics (the indirect object) and omit the word *to*. Study the first two examples carefully.

1. Fred gave the money to *me*. —<u>Fred gave me the money.</u>
2. I wrote a letter to *Mr. Holt*. —<u>I wrote Mr. Holt a letter.</u>
3. The agent sold the house to *Mr. and Mrs. Hanson*.
4. We gave a birthday present to *Martha* yesterday.
5. Mr. Johnson sent a letter to *the Jiffy Company*.
6. Did the boy throw the baseball to *his friend*?
7. Tom handed the books and envelopes to *me*.
8. Miss Wilson sent some beautiful flowers to *us*.
9. Mrs. Baker wrote a letter to *her son* last Friday.
10. Please give your paper to *me* right now.
11. Our friends sent the package to *us* the next day.
12. The teacher told an interesting story to *the students*.
13. I showed all of the photographs to *my friends*.
14. Professor Moore gave some excellent advice to *all of us*.

PART TWO : THE INDIRECT OBJECT WITHOUT TO

Change the position of the word or words in italics (the indirect object) and add the word *to*. Study the first two examples carefully.

1. I told *him* the story. —<u>I told the story to him.</u>
2. We wrote *them* a letter. —<u>We wrote a letter to them.</u>
3. Dr. Davis gave *Charles* the tickets.
4. Did the manager offer *that fellow* the job?
5. Mr. Meyer told *us* the story of his narrow escape.
6. Louise and Betty sent *Mary* a birthday gift last week.
7. Did Mr. Kennedy lend *his brother* the money?
8. Mrs. Garcia told *us* an interesting story last night.
9. Are you going to write *George* a letter soon?
10. Please lend *me* your pen and pencil for a few minutes.
11. My wife sent *them* the package last Thursday or Friday.
12. The Bakers read *us* all of those interesting letters.
13. Are you going to show *the people* your photographs tonight?
14. Mr. and Mrs. Brown mailed *us* a lovely gift from Mexico.

HEARING AND SPEAKING LESSON

PART ONE : THE INDIRECT OBJECT WITH TO

Listen carefully. Answer the questions with a full sentence.

1. *Fred gave me the money.*
2. *I wrote Mr. Holt a letter.*
3.
4.
5.
6.
7.
8.
9.
10.
11.
12.
13.
14.

PART TWO : THE INDIRECT OBJECT WITHOUT TO

Listen carefully. Answer the questions with a full sentence.

1. *I told the story to him.*
2. *We wrote a letter to them.*
3.
4.
5.
6.
7.
8.
9.
10.
11.
12.
13.
14.

REVIEW : THE PRESENT TENSES

Write the correct form of the verb in parentheses in each sentence. Use only the simple present tense (examples : *he works, they study*) or the continuous present tense(examples : *he is working, they are studying*).

1. I often (*leave*) town over the weekend.
2. Miss Peters (*use*) the telephone now.
3. The children always (*go*) to bed early.
4. Mrs. Johnson (*prepare*) dinner now.
5. Look! That boy (*run*) into the house.
6. Miss Melnick (*understand*) those words.
7. The students (*finish*) their papers now.
8. I (*need*) some money for my textbooks.
9. The guests (*watch*) that television program now.
10. We (*review*) the use of the tenses in English this week.
11. Yes, Marjorie (*want*) some cake and coffee.
12. I (*go*) to bed around eleven o'clock during the week.
13. We never (*go*) to the library in the evening.
14. Mr. Harris (*teach*) English from 2:00 to 5:00 p.m.
15. Mr. and Mrs. Stewart (*fly*) to California every winter.
16. Daniel Soto (*work*) thirty-eight hours a week.
17. I (*hear*) the sound of a motor outside!
18. Our English class always (*start*) at 8:30 p.m.
19. I (*read*) an interesting book about the Civil War.
20. Mr. Smith's secretary (*sit*) at another desk today.
21. The weather (*get*) very hot here in July and August.
22. My friend (*study*) his English lesson one hour every night.
23. Mr. Rockwell (*pay*) his bills at the end of every month.
24. That tall fellow in my class (*come*) from Greece.
25. Professor Moore (*write*) another book about English.
26. It (*rain*) very much in this region in the spring.
27. Frank (*have*) a bad cold. He (*take*) some medicine for it.
28. That department store (*have*) a big sale on shoes today.
29. Listen! I (*think*) someone (*knock*) at the front door.
30. I (*see*) the airplane now. It (*come*) in this direction.
31. Mr. Berg always (*do*) his English lessons very carefully.
32. The students (*do*) Exercise 69 on page 114 right now.

HEARING AND SPEAKING LESSON

Listen carefully. Answer the questions with a full sentence.

1. *I often leave town over the weekend.*
2. *Miss Peters is using the telephone now.*
3.
4.
5.
6.
7.
8.
9.
10.
11.
12.
13.
14.
15.
16.
17.
18.
19.
20.
21.
22.
23.
24.
25.
26.
27.
28.
29.
30.
31.
32.

REVIEW : QUESTIONS WITH BE AND WILL   70

Change the following statements to simple questions. Notice the examples.

1. That man is Mr. Harris. —*Is that man Mr. Harris?*
2. There are chairs in that room. —*Are there chairs in that room?*
3. He is studying right now. —*Is he studying right now?*
4. They will return soon. —*Will they return soon?*
5. The last lesson was very difficult for the students.
6. Mr. Meyer is listening to the radio right now.
7. The Andersons will travel to South America by air.
8. Alice is taking a course in history this semester.
9. Mr. and Mrs. Kennedy are going to stay at a hotel.
10. There were a lot of people at the party last night.
11. His friends will get the train at Grand Central Station.
12. The men were very tired after all of the hard work.
13. Miss Stewart is going to be busy this afternoon.
14. There will be a meeting here next Thursday night.

REVIEW : QUESTIONS WITH DO   71

Change the following statements to simple questions. Notice the examples.

1. Fred drives carefully. —*Does Fred drive carefully?*
2. They study every evening. —*Do they study every evening?*
3. She bought a new dress. —*Did she buy a new dress?*
4. Mr. Harper walked downtown with his friend.
5. The students in that class always work very hard.
6. Mr. Williams knows Professor Moore very well.
7. Tom's friend finished all of the work for him.
8. Miss Stewart wore her new spring dress yesterday.
9. The students had trouble with the first part of the lesson.
10. Martha does her homework for this class in the evening.
11. The two plumbers did the work in the basement quickly.
12. Mr. Berg always comes to this class on time.
13. Miss Cunningham put the money in the top desk drawer.
14. All of the students understand the last two lessons.

HEARING AND SPEAKING LESSON 70

Listen carefully. Answer the questions with a full sentence.

1. *Is that man Mr. Harris?*
2. *Are there chairs in that room?*
3.
4.
5.
6.
7.
8.
9.
10.
11.
12.
13.
14.

HEARING AND SPEAKING LESSON 71

Listen carefully. Answer the questions with a full sentence.

1. *Does Fred drive carefully?*
2. *Do they study every evening?*
3.
4.
5.
6.
7.
8.
9.
10.
11.
12.
13.
14.

REVIEW : WRITING QUESTIONS   72

Change the following statements to simple questions.

1. The men are waiting in the other room now.
2. Carol learned all of the new words by heart.
3. Our teacher will explain that lesson to us tomorrow.
4. That department store is having a big sale today.
5. Mr. and Mrs. Hanson are going to write to us from Italy.
6. Mr. Kennedy usually leaves his car in the alley.
7. The students are copying the sentences from the blackboard.
8. That fellow lost his temper during the argument.
9. The mechanic did all of the work very carefully.
10. The students' papers will be on Mr. Crowell's desk.
11. Your friend had a good time at the party last night.
12. The men will finish all of their work before next Friday.
13. Mrs. Wilson took her sister downtown in her car.
14. His secretary sent the letter to that company by airmail.

REVIEW : WRITING NEGATIVES   73

Change the following statements to negatives. Study the examples carefully.

1. Frank knows that word. —*Frank doesn't know that word.*
2. Tom is studying his lesson now. —*Tom isn't studying his lesson now.*
3. He will be there tomorrow. —*He won't be there tomorrow.*
4. There were many people at the meeting yesterday.
5. My friend always studies his lessons at the library.
6. Mr. Harris taught this same English class last year.
7. Fred's cousin will get back here before two-thirty.
8. Professor Moore put some papers on his desk.
9. The students are talking to their teacher right now.
10. Daniel Soto does his English lessons in the afternoon.
11. You had the right answer to that question on your paper.
12. Mr. Johnson's secretary is writing letters for him right now.
13. I am working on my English assignment right now.
14. Mrs. Franklin called her friend and told her the news.
15. My assistant will have enough time for that this week.

HEARING AND SPEAKING LESSON 72

Listen carefully. Answer the questions with a full sentence.

1. *Are the men waiting in the other room now?*
2. *Did Carol learn all of the new words by heart?*
3.
4.
5.
6.
7.
8.
9.
10.
11.
12.
13.
14.

HEARING AND SPEAKING LESSON 73

Listen carefully. Answer the questions with a full sentence.

1. *Frank doesn't know that word.*
2. *Tom isn't studying his lesson now.*
3.
4.
5.
6.
7.
8.
9.
10.
11.
12.
13.
14.
15.

SHORT ANSWERS TO QUESTIONS 74

Give short answers to these questions. Use personal pronouns (*you, it, they, etc.*) or *there* in the short answer. Use contractions only for short answers with *no*.

QUESTION

1. Is Mrs. Smith in the other room?
2. Does the man like strong coffee?
3. Will you be ready before three o'clock?
4. Is there going to be a meeting tonight?
5. Is the alarm clock ringing right now?
6. Are the students ready for the test?
7. Do these students work very hard?
8. Were the last two lessons difficult?
9. Do you want a cheese sandwich?
10. Was there a book on Mr. Crowell's desk?
11. Did Mrs. Burke's sister go with you?
12. Will Marjorie answer the phone for us?
13. Did the men move the furniture?
14. Are you going to study German?
15. Were there many people at the concert?
16. Do you know the answer to that question?
17. Does the bus stop at the next corner?
18. Will Dr. Duncan's speech be interesting?
19. Did that woman find her purse?
20. Was there a chair in the other room?
21. Will the Browns travel to Spain by boat?
22. Is the weather warm in the spring?
23. Are you working on your assignment?
24. Does Mr. Berg study every night?
25. Will this be enough money for everything?
26. Were there enough sandwiches on the plate?
27. Do your friends like the United States?
28. Did the women attend the meeting?
29. Are the children sleeping right now?
30. Was this a very difficult assignment?

HEARING AND SPEAKING LESSON 🔊   **74**

Listen carefully. Answer the questions with a full sentence.

SHORT ANSWER

1. Yes, *she is. Mrs. Smith is in the room.*
2. No, *he doesn't. The man doesn't like strong coffee.*
3. No, *I won't.*
4. Yes,
5. No,
6. Yes,
7. No,
8. Yes,
9. Yes,
10. No,
11. Yes,
12. Yes,
13. No,
14. No,
15. Yes,
16. No,
17. Yes,
18. Yes,
19. No,
20. No,
21. No,
22. Yes,
23. Yes,
24. No,
25. Yes,
26. No,
27. Yes,
28. No,
29. Yes,
30. No,

FREE WRITING PRACTICE(8)

dining room

What can you see in this picture?

I can see a dining table.
I can see chairs.

What are they doing?

they are eating their dinner.

What are on the dining table?

FREE WRITING PRACTICE(9)

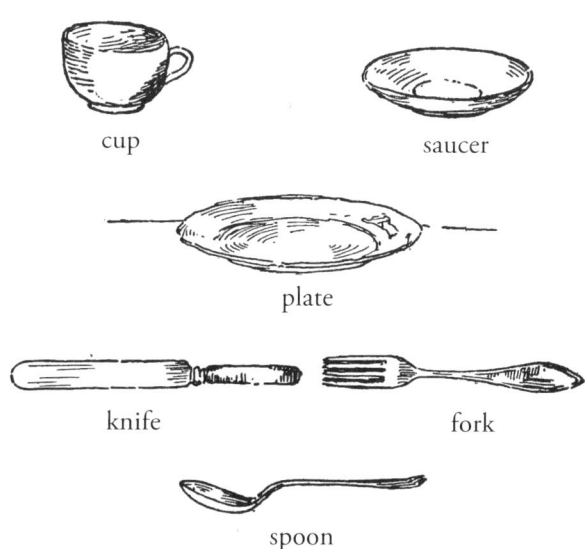

cup

saucer

plate

knife

fork

spoon

there are cups on the table.

there are saucers on the table.

there are plates on the table.

there are knives on the table.

there are forks on the table.

there are spoons on the table

"WILLIAM HOWARD HOLT"

William Howard Holt was born in Chicago in 1956. He lived there with his parents until 1962. Then his parents moved to Detroit. He and his two brothers finished elementary school in Detroit. He finished in 1970. His father started a business in New York the next year. Therefore, he attended high school in that city. He went to Bryant High School for four years. He received his diploma in 1974. Unfortunately, he didn't have enough money for a university education. His first job was in the office of a shoe company. He worked there for two years. He was the assistant bookkeeper. He married Miss Marie Stoddard in 1975. In 1976, he became a salesperson for a metal products company. He didn't enjoy that job at all. Therefore, he quit the job six months later. He and his wife moved to Florida that year, and he found a job. He started his own business in Miami in 1978. Unfortunately, his business failed after only six months. He lost almost $20,000. Then he was sales manager for a small container corporation for six years. Between 1977 and 1984, Mr. Holt and his wife had four children. The first child was born in 1977, and the last child was born in 1983. In 1986, Mr. Holt started another business. He called his business the Jiffy Box Company. His business was very successful, and he made a lot of money. He and his wife traveled to Cuba, Venezuela, Colombia, Brazil, and other South American countries several times between 1992 and 1994. He learned Spanish very well during that time. Their oldest son, Thomas, went to Purdue University in 1996. Mr. Holt retired from active business life in 2000. After that, he and his wife moved to Europe for four years. Their daughter Marjorie lived in Europe with them for a year. She learned French in only six months. Their other two sons graduated from the University of Wisconsin in 2003 and 2004. Thomas got married in 2000 and has two children now. Marjorie is still going to school. She is working for an advanced degree at Michigan State University. Mr. Holt is going to school now too. He is going to a university because he wants to complete his education. He started two years ago. He will finish his university degree two years from now.

HEARING AND SPEAKING LESSON

Listen carefully. How do you read year expressions such as 1956, 1962?

1956 : nineteen fifty six
1962 : nineteen sixty two
1970 :
1974 :
1975 :
1976 :
1978 :
1983 :
1984 :
1992 :
1994 :
1999 :
2000 :
2001 :
2002 :
2010 :
2012 :

QUESTIONS ABOUT MR. HOLT'S LIFE 76

Answer the following questions about the story on the previous page.

1 Where was William Howard Holt born? **2** When was he born? **3** How long did he live in Chicago? **4** Where did he finish elementary school? **5** When did he finish elementary school? **6** Where did he go in 1971? **7** In what city did he go to high school? **8** Why did he attend high school in New York? **9** What high school did he attend? **10** When did he receive his diploma? **11** Why didn't he go to a university? **12** Where was his first job? **13** How long did he work for the shoe company? **14** What was his position in that company? **15** Whom did he marry? **16** What was his wife's maiden name? **17** When did he marry her? **18** What did he do after that? **19** What kind of company did he work for? **20** What did he do for that company? **21** How did he like his job as a salesman? **22** How many months did he work as a salesman? **23** Where did he move after that? **24** What state did he and his wife move to? **25** When did he start his own business? **26** Where did he start his own business? **27** When did his business fail? **28** How much money did he lose? **29** What kind of company did he work for next? **30** How long did he work for that company? **31** When was the Holts' first child born? **32** When were their other children born? **33** How many children do the Holts have in all? **34** What did Mr. Holt do in 1986? **35** What did he name his business? **36** How did his business do? **37** What countries did the Holts visit in South America? **38** When did they go there? **39** When did Mr. Holt learn Spanish? **40** Where did Thomas go in 1996? **41** When did Mr. Holt retire from active business life? **42** Where did the Holts move then? **43** When did the Holts move to Europe? **44** Who went to Europe with them? **45** Where were the other children? **46** How long did Marjorie live in Europe with them? **47** What language did Marjorie learn? **48** How long did it take her? **49** When did their two other sons graduate from the University of Wisconsin? **50** When did Thomas get married? **51** How many children do Thomas and his wife have now? **52** Where is Marjorie going to school? **53** What is Mr. Holt doing at present? **54** When will he finish his university degree?

HEARING AND SPEAKING LESSON

Listen carefully. Answer the questions with a full sentence.

1 *He was born in Chicago.*   2 *He was born in 1956.*   3 ....
4 ....   5 ....
6 ....   7 ....
8 ....   9 ....
10 ....   11 ....
12 ....   13 ....   14 ....
15 ....   16 ....
17 ....   18 ....
19 ....   20 ....
21 ....   22 ....
23 ....   24 ....
25 ....   26 ....
27 ....   28 ....   29 ....
30 ....
31 ....   32 ....
33 ....   34 ....
35 ....   36 ....
37 ....   38 ....
39 ....   40 ....
41 ....   42 ....
43 ....   44 ....
45 ....   46 ....
47 ....   48 ....
49 ....   50 ....
51 ....
52 ....   53 ....
54 ....

QUESTIONS ABOUT YOUR ENGLISH CLASS

Answer these questions about your English class. Read the questions carefully. Notice the position of all the words in the question. Compare the position of the words in the question with the position of the words in your answer.

1 Why are you studying English? **2** Why did you choose this school? **3** When did you start your English course? **4** How long ago did you start your class in English? **5** At what school are you studying English now? **6** Where did you study English before this? **7** How many years did you study English before this? **8** What is your teacher's name? **9** Who is your teacher? **10** How do you like your English class? **11** What is the name of your textbook? **12** At what time does your English class begin? **13** How long does your English class last? **14** How long is each class period? **15** What do you do during the first ten minutes? **16** What are you doing right now? **17** What is your teacher talking about right now? **18** At what time is your class over? **19** How many classes do you attend each week? **20** What lesson are you studying this week? **21** When do you usually study your homework? **22** How much time do you spend on your homework? **23** Whom do you study your lessons with? **24** With whom do you practice pronunciation? **25** How many sentences do you write every day? **26** What did your teacher talk about yesterday? **27** What is your teacher going to talk about tomorrow? **28** How many hours are you going to study at home next week? **29** How often do you speak English outside of this class? **30** When is your teacher going to give an examination? **31** Which lesson was the most difficult for you? **32** What things give you the most trouble? **33** Why do these things give you trouble? **34** How many new words did you learn yesterday? **35** How many English words do you know in all? **36** How many exercises are there in this book? **37** How many pages are there in this book? **38** How many mistakes did you make on the last exercise? **39** How often does your teacher dictate sentences to you? **40** How often does your teacher give you a vocabulary test? **41** How many exercises does your teacher assign each week? **42** How often do you write letters in English? **43** Which exercise are you writing right now? **44** At what time did you get to school today? **45** How did you get to school today? **46** How do you usually get to school? **47** Who sits beside you in your classroom?

HEARING AND SPEAKING LESSON

Listen carefully. Answer the questions with a full sentence.

1 *I am studying English because...* **2** *I chose this school because...* **3** ....
.... **4** ....
5 .... **6** ....
.... **7** .... **8** ....
.... **9** .... **10** .... **11** ....
.... **12** ....
13 .... **14** .... **15** ......
.... **16** .... **17** ....
.... **18** ....
19 .... **20** ....
.... **21** .... **22** ....
.... **23** .... **24** ....
.... **25** ....
.... **26** .... **27** ....
.... **28** ....
.... **29** .... **30** ....
.... **31** ....
32 .... **33** ....
.... **34** .... **35** ....
.... **36** .... **37** ....
.... **38** ....
.... **39** .... **40** ....
.... **41** ....
.... **42** .... **43** ....
.... **44** ....
.... **45** .... **46** ....
47 ....

QUESTIONS ABOUT YOUR LIFE

Answer these questions about your life. Read the questions carefully. Notice the use of the question words (*when, why, how, how many, how long, etc.*)

1 When were you born? **2** How old are you now? **3** In what city were you born? **4** What country do you come from? **5** What is your native language? **6** Where did you go to elementary school? **7** What other schools did you go to? **8** How long did you study English in your country? **9** How big is your family? **10** Where do the other members of your family live? **11** How many brothers and sisters do you have? **12** How long did you attend your last school? **13** What subjects did you study? **14** What was your favorite subject? **15** When did you get married? **16** What is your wife's (husband's) name? **17** How many children do you have? **18** Why did you leave your country? **19** When did you arrive in the United States? **20** Where did you live during 2002 World Cup? **21** At what school are you studying English? **22** Why did you choose this school? **23** How well do you speak and write English? **24** How long are you going to stay in this country? **25** How long are you going to study English? **26** Where do you live? **27** What is your address? **28** Who is your best friend? **29** With whom do you live? **30** Which city do you prefer, this city or your hometown? **31** What is your profession at this moment? **32** What do you plan to do in the future? **33** Why do you want to do that? **34** Where do you usually go over the weekend? **35** What do you usually do on Saturday and Sunday? **36** What did you do last weekend? **37** What are you going to do next weekend? **38** What is your favorite sport? **39** What is your hobby? **40** How much time do you spend on your hobby each week? **41** In which bank do you keep your money? **42** How many friends do you have in this city? **43** How many of the students in your English class do you know? **44** When did you have your last vacation? **45** When are you going to take your next vacation? **46** Where are you going to go on your vacation? **47** What are you going to do after this semester? **48** At what time do you usually get up in the morning? **49** At what time do you get up on Saturday and Sunday? **50** What kind of breakfast do you usually eat? **51** At what time do you usually leave home? **52** How do you usually get to work (or school)? **53** Where do you generally eat lunch?

HEARING AND SPEAKING LESSON 🔊

Listen carefully. Answer the questions with a full sentence.

1 *I was born in 1977.* **2** *I am 35 years old now.* **3** .... **4** ....
5 .... **6** ....
7 .... **8** ....
9 .... **10** ....
11 ....
12 .... **13** .... **14** ....
15 .... **16** ....
17 .... **18** ....
19 .... **20** ....
21 .... **22** ....
23 ....
24 .... **25** ....
26 .... **27** .... **28** ....
29 .... **30** ....
31 .... **32** ....
33 .... **34** ....
35 .... **36** ....
37 .... **38** ....
39 .... **40** ....
41 .... **42** ....
43 ....
44 .... **45** ....
46 .... **47** ....
48 ....
49 .... **50** ....
51 ....
52 .... **53** ....
....

USING THE QUESTION WORDS (1) — 79

Choose *where*, *when*, or *why* for each question. Read the short answer at the right. Then choose the appropriate question word.

	QUESTION	ANSWER
1	---- did you put your books?	On the desk.
2	---- did you speak to Mr. Adams?	Two days ago.
3	---- do you need the money now?	To buy a suit.
4	---- will they arrive at the airport?	About ten o'clock.
5	---- did that accident happen?	At the intersection.
6	---- are you going to go home now?	Because it's late.
7	---- do you keep your car?	In our garage.
8	---- did you go to the library?	To get a book.
9	---- does summer start in this country?	On June 21.
10	---- were you late for class today?	I missed my bus.
11	---- will you spend your vacation?	In New England.
12	---- are you going to tell them the news?	Tomorrow night.
13	---- is a payphone in this building?	Beside the elevator.
14	---- are you taking a course in English?	I need practice.

WRITING QUESTIONS WITH WHY — 80

(a) Change each statement to a simple question, (b) Change the simple question to a question with the word *why*. Study the first example.

1 Martha went downtown yesterday.

   (a) *Did Martha go downtown yesterday?*

   (b) *Why did she go there yesterday?*

2 John borrowed a dictionary from Bill.
3 The Andersons are going to travel by train.
4 Mr. Slater sold his house in North Plains.
5 Those two men were late for work today.
6 Mr. Moore usually comes to school by bus.
7 That student spoke to the teacher after class.
8 They sent the letters to the wrong address.
9 Your friend took those two books back to the library.
10 Marjorie called her sister and told her the news.
11 Mr. Meyer will be absent from his English class tomorrow.
12 Bill gets off the bus there and transfers to another one.
13 I'm going to leave my house early tomorrow morning.

HEARING AND SPEAKING LESSON 🔊 79

Listen carefully. Answer the questions with a full sentence.

	QUESTION	ANSWER
1	*Where did you put your book?*	*I put my books on the desk.*
2	*When did you speak to Mr. Adam?*	*I spoke to Mr. Adam two days ago.*
3		
4		
5		
6		
7		
8		
9		
10		
11		
12		
13		
14		

HEARING AND SPEAKING LESSON 🔊 80

Listen carefully. Answer the questions with a full sentence.

1 *(a) Did Martha go downtown yesterday? (b) Why did she go there yesterday?*
2 *(a) Did John borrow a dictionary from Bill? (b) Why did he borrow it from Bill?*
3
4
5
6
7
8
9
10
11
12
13

"THE EXECUTIVE'S DAY" 81

Read this schedule carefully. Then answer the questions in the next exercise. For additional practice, change all of the verbs in the schedule to the past tense.

He gets up at 7:30 in the morning. He takes a shower at 7:45 a.m. He gets dressed at 8:00 a.m. He eats his breakfast at 8:20 a.m. He leaves for the office at 8:40 a.m. He takes a taxi at the corner at 8:45 a.m. He gets to the office at 9:00 a.m. He dictates letters to his secretary at 9:30 a.m. He reads the morning mail at 10:00 a.m. He goes out for coffee at 10:30 a.m. He returns to the office at 11:00 a.m. He has a conference with the other executives at 11:30 a.m. He leaves the office at 12:30 p.m He has his lunch at the Plaza Hotel at 1:00 p.m. He returns to his office at 1:30 p.m. He calls his secretary into his office at 1:45 p.m. He dictates answers to the morning mail at 1:45 p.m. He meets important visitors between 2:00 p.m. and 3:00 p.m. He discusses problems with his two assistants between 3:00 p.m. and 3:30 p.m. He makes most of his important telephone calls after 3:30 p.m. He goes over the company reports between 4:00 p.m. and 4:30 p.m. He catches a taxi in front of his office at 5:45 p.m. He gets back home at 6:00 p.m. He eats dinner with his wife and children at 6:30 p.m. He reads the evening newspaper between 7:30 p.m. and 8:30 p.m.

QUESTIONS ABOUT "THE EXECUTIVE'S DAY" 82

Supply the correct words for the blank spaces in each question. Note: In this type of question, the word *at* is often omitted.

1. At what time *does he get up* in the morning? *He gets up at 7:30 in the morning.*
2. At what time ---- ---- ---- a shower?
3. At what time ---- ---- ---- his breakfast?
4. At what time ---- ---- ---- for his office?
5. At what time ---- ---- ---- a taxi at the corner?
6. At what time ---- ---- ---- to the office?
7. At what time ---- ---- ---- letters to his secretary?
8. At what time ---- ---- ---- his lunch at the hotel?
9. At what time ---- ---- ---- answers to the mail?
10. At what time ---- ---- ---- important visitors?
11. At what time ---- ---- ---- his telephone calls?
12. At what time ---- ---- ---- the company reports?
13. At what time ---- ---- ---- the evening newspaper?
14. At what time ---- ---- ---- dinner with his family?

HEARING AND SPEAKING LESSON 81

Listen carefully. How do you read time expressions such as 7:30, 7:45?

7:30 : seven thrity or half past seven
7:45 : seven forty-five or a quarter to eight.

HEARING AND SPEAKING LESSON 82

Listen carefully. Answer the questions with a full sentence.

1 *At what time does he get up in the morning? He gets up at 7:30 in the morning.*
2 *At what time does he take a shower? He takes a shower at 7:45 a.m.*
3
4
5
6
7
8
9
10
11
12
13
14

WHO, WHOM, WHOSE, WHAT, WHICH

Study these questions and short answers carefully. Pay special attention to the order of words. Some of the questions have statement word order. Indicate with a check the questions with statement word order.

	QUESTION	ANSWER
1	Who invited George to dinner?	The Taylors.
2	Who(m) did the Taylors invite to dinner?	George.
3	What did the Taylors serve for dinner?	Roast beef.
4	What happened after dinner?	Nothing special.
5	Who used Mr. Berg's dictionary in class?	Mr. Kramer.
6	Whose dictionary did Mr. Kramer use in class?	Mr. Berg's.
7	Whose dictionary is on my desk?	Mine.
8	Which dictionary is yours? There are two.	The small one.
9	What is the name of your dictionary?	"Word Guide."
10	Who is going to speak to Dr. Duncan?	I am.
11	Who(m) are you going to speak to?	Dr. Duncan.
12	To whom is Mr. Burke going to send a letter?	To the editor.
13	Who is going to send a letter to the editor?	Mr. Burke.
14	What is Mr. Burke going to send to the editor?	A letter.
15	What supplies the power for this motor?	A generator.
16	Who supplies the electricity for this building?	The Electric Co.
17	What color did you paint your house?	Blue and white.
18	Which color did you use the most?	White.
19	Who sent that package to Miss Davis?	I sent it.
20	To whom did you send that package?	To Miss Davis.
21	What did you send to Miss Davis?	That package.
22	Whose books are on that table?	Dick's.
23	Which is Tom's, the red one or the blue one?	The red one.
24	Who(m) did your friends meet at the corner?	Mr. Kennedy.
25	With whom did your friends ride to school?	With Mr. Fox.
26	Who(m) did they ride downtown with?	With George.
27	Who drove them back home afterwards?	George.
28	What kind of car does George have?	A Ford.
29	What model does he have?	The new one.
30	Whose car is in front of your house now?	Mr. Kennedy's.

HEARING AND SPEAKING LESSON

Listen carefully. Answer the questions with a full sentence.

ANSWER
1. The Taylors invited George to dinner.
2. George is who(m) the Taylors invited to dinner.
3. The Taylors served roast beef for dinner.
4. Nothing special happended after dinner.
5. Mr. Kramer used Mr. Berg's doctionary.

QUESTIONS WITH HOW — 84

Study these questions with how. Notice the short answers at the right.

QUESTION	ANSWER
1 How did you do that work?	With some tools.
2 How is the weather today?	Quite chilly.
3 How often do you watch television?	Twice a week.
4 How did you get here this morning?	By bus.
5 How do you like the weather here?	Very much.
6 How long will you stay in Detroit?	Two months.
7 How many students are there here?	Twenty-one.
8 How much coffee did you drink today?	Three cups.

ADJECTIVES WITH HOW — 85

Use adjectives (*big, cold, often, far, long, etc.*) after how in these questions.

1 How ---- will your friends stay in New York?
2 How ---- is your classroom (in square feet)?
3 How ---- is New York from San Francisco?
4 How ---- does it get in June, July, and August?
5 How ---- is the Empire State Building in New York?
6 How ---- do you go to concerts or lectures?
7 How ---- is your English teacher?
8 How ---- were the last two reading assignments?

MUCH AND MANY WITH HOW — 86

Use *much* or *many* after *how* in each of these sentences.

1 How ---- students are there in your English class?
2 How ---- bread is there in the kitchen?
3 How ---- letters do you write to your parents each week?
4 How ---- sugar do you want in your coffee?
5 How ---- cups of coffee did you drink during the day?
6 How ---- did you pay for your new winter overcoat?
7 How ---- times did you write the words on the list?
8 How ---- time do you spend on your homework?

HEARING AND SPEAKING LESSON 84

Listen carefully. Answer the questions with a full sentence.

ANSWER
1. *I did that work with some tools.*
2. *The weather is quite chilly today.*
3.
4.
5.
6.
7.
8.

HEARING AND SPEAKING LESSON 85

Listen carefully. Answer the questions with a full sentence.

1. *How long will your friends stay in New York? They will stay in New York for 2 weeks.*
2. *How big is your classroom? My classroom is 900 squar feet.*
3.
4.
5.
6.
7.
8.

HEARING AND SPEAKING LESSON 86

Listen carefully. Answer the questions with a full sentence.

1. *How many students are there in your classroom? There are 15 students in my classroom.*
2. *How much bread is there in the kitchen? There are 2 loafs of bread in the kitchen.*
3.
4.
5.
6.
7.
8.

USING THE QUESTION WORDS(2)

Read the answer to the question. Then supply the appropriate question word (*why, who, which, how far, etc.*) in the blank space in each sentence.

	QUESTION	ANSWER
1	---- are you going now?	To the library.
2	---- English book is this?	My English book.
3	---- time is it now?	It's eight-fifteen.
4	---- money do you have?	Seventy-five cents.
5	---- one did Bill take?	The small one.
6	---- was that tall boy?	My friend, Frank.
7	---- did you talk to?	The chairman.
8	---- is your brother?	Twenty years old.
9	---- flour did you buy?	Two pounds.
10	---- did you get to school?	By car.
11	---- girl is your sister?	The thin one.
12	---- color is her hair?	Light brown.
13	---- will she get here?	Probably Monday.
14	---- do they come here?	Twice a year.
15	---- does "peculiar" mean?	It means "strange."
16	---- is a bus stop?	At the next corner.
17	---- put the chair here?	Roger, I think.
18	---- are you going to buy?	A pair of shoes.
19	---- is Fred talking to now?	Mr. Kennedy.
20	---- were you in the army?	Three years.
21	---- did you meet yesterday?	Betty's cousin.
22	---- do you do that?	Because I enjoy it.
23	---- is Miami from there?	A hundred miles.
24	---- people are there here?	About thirty-five.
25	---- do you want your coffee?	With cream.
26	---- will you get to Chicago?	By air.
27	---- do you travel so much?	I like it.
28	---- will you be in Venezuela?	Several months.
29	---- is your brother?	Five feet eleven.
30	---- kind of cloth is that?	It's silk.

HEARING AND SPEAKING LESSON

Listen carefully. Answer the questions with a full sentence.

	QUESTION	ANSWER
1	Where are you going now?	I am going to the library.
2	Whose English book is this?	This is my English book.
3		
4		
5		
6		
7		
8		
9		
10		
11		
12		
13		
14		
15		
16		
17		
18		
19		
20		
21		
22		
23		
24		
25		
26		
27		
28		
29		
30		

USING THE QUESTION WORDS(3)

Read the answer to the question. Then supply the appropriate question word(*what, whose, when, how much, etc.*) in the blank space in each sentence.

	QUESTION	ANSWER
1	---- did you put my book?	On the desk.
2	---- does your school start?	In September.
3	---- gave Mr. Green the money?	His sister.
4	---- did he need the money?	To buy a ticket.
5	---- books are these?	Jim's.
6	---- are your friends now?	At Jim's house.
7	---- did Smith leave for Boston?	Last Friday.
8	---- is it to Los Angeles from here?	Fifty-five miles.
9	---- is going to help you tonight?	My friend Bill.
10	---- is he going to help?	All of us.
11	---- did Mr. Brown say to you?	Nothing important.
12	---- dictionary will you use?	Mr. Meyer's.
13	---- cups of coffee did you drink?	Two or three.
14	---- color did you paint your house?	White.
15	---- gasoline do you need?	Ten gallons.
16	---- did you go there yesterday?	To see Thomas.
17	---- of these do you prefer?	That one.
18	---- kind of material is that?	It's wool.
19	---- did the accident happen?	At the corner.
20	---- is the nickname for "Robert?"	It's "Bob."
21	---- did you speak to Mr. Berg?	Yesterday.
22	---- did you pay for that suit?	Sixty dollars.
23	---- does that word mean?	It means "easy."
24	---- ago did Mr. Johnson leave?	A week ago.
25	---- are your friends leaving now?	Because it's late.
26	---- one did you finally buy?	The red one.
27	---- do you want to get it now?	I need it.
28	---- do you like this city?	Very well.
29	---- do you call that in English?	A "suitcase."
30	---- do you pronounce that word?	Like this.

HEARING AND SPEAKING LESSON

Listen carefully. Answer the questions with a full sentence.

	QUESTION	ANSWER
1	*Where did you put my book?*	*I put your book on the desk.*
2	*When does your school start?*	*My school starts in September.*
3		
4		
5		
6		
7		
8		
9		
10		
11		
12		
13		
14		
15		
16		
17		
18		
19		
20		
21		
22		
23		
24		
25		
26		
27		
28		
29		
30		

FREE WRITING PRACTICE(10)

cup   glass

What can you do with this cup or glass?

I have a glass.

I drink a glass of water.

I drink water from a glass.

We do not drink coffee from a glass.

I have a cup.

I drink a cup of coffee.

I drink coffee from a cup.

We do not drink water from a cup.

FREE WRITING PRACTICE(11)

knife   fork   spoon

I have a knife, fork and spoon.

I cut with a knife.

I cannot cut with a fork.

I cannot cut with a spoon.

I eat with a fork and spoon.

I stir the coffee with a spoon.

I do not stir the coffee with a fork.

ASKING FOR INFORMATION(1)

Write a question about the italicized part of each sentence. Begin each question with a question word (*where, what, how much, etc.*). Notice the examples.

1. Alice went *to the movies* last night. —<u>Where did Alice go last night?</u>
2. They will be there *for two weeks*. —<u>How long will they be there?</u>
3. *Miss Peters* wrote those letters. —<u>Who wrote those letters?</u>
4. Bill's birthday is *on the twelfth of August.*
5. There are *twenty-one floors* in that building.
6. John is coughing *because he has a bad cold.*
7. The Browns left for home *at six o'clock.*
8. The students studied *the irregular verbs.*
9. That is *Professor Moore's* briefcase.
10. There were *fourteen guests* at the party.
11. Mr. Burke bought his new car *last Saturday.*
12. Detroit is *seven hundred miles from* there.
13. Their classes usually begin *at nine o'clock.*
14. I'm going to go *because the game will be interesting.*
15. That customer wants *four packages* of cigarettes.
16. Dorothy bought *the pink dress* with the blue stripes.
17. We call those things "*gadgets*" in English.
18. My friends helped me *very* much yesterday afternoon.
19. *Mr. Wilson* gave the annual report to Mr. Johnson.
20. The whole trip takes about *twenty-two hours.*
21. We're going to look for *winter coats* at that department store.
22. Those two dictionaries belong to *Mr. Kramer.*
23. Our friends stayed in California *for three weeks.*
24. The messenger gave the packages to *Mr. Wilson's secretary.*
25. Mother put the cups and saucers *in the cupboard.*
26. The word "rapid" means "*fast*" or "*quick.*"
27. The doctor will come *within fifteen or twenty minutes.*
28. The price of that car is *three thousand dollars.*
29. Dr. Duncan's mother is *sixty-eight years* old.
30. There will be another meeting *next Thursday or Friday.*
31. Edward has about *two thousand dollars* in the bank now.
32. Mr. Green wrote to his brother *because he needed some money.*

HEARING AND SPEAKING LESSON 🔊

Listen carefully. Answer the questions with a full sentence.

1. *Where did Alice go last night?*
2. *How long will they be there?*
3.
4.
5.
6.
7.
8.
9.
10.
11.
12.
13.
14.
15.
16.
17.
18.
19.
20.
21.
22.
23.
24.
25.
26.
27.
28.
29.
30.
31.
32.

ASKING FOR INFORMATION(2)

Write a question about the italicized part of each sentence. Begin each question with a question word (*who, why, how many, etc.*). Notice the examples.

1. The Holts have *four* children. —<u>How many children do the Holts have?</u>
2. The accident happened *right there*. —<u>Where did the accident happen?</u>
3. Mr. and Mrs. Hanson are going to go *to Brazil* next year.
4. Their guests left for home *because it was very late*.
5. Our classroom is *twenty-eight feet* wide.
6. It's about *twelve blocks* to the post office from here.
7. The two men returned to the office *at three o'clock*.
8. That modern chair costs *forty-four dollars plus tax*.
9. The secretary gave Mr. Green *a lot of* information.
10. The name of that book by Mark Twain is "*Tom Sawyer.*"
11. Mr. and Mrs. Smith will return to New York *by train*.
12. *The tall man* on the left is Mr. Brown's brother.
13. Those two students are talking about *the last lesson*.
14. Mr. Kennedy will leave for Baltimore *after the holidays*.
15. Miss Stewart chose *the black dress with the lace*.
16. Her sister bought *three pairs* of stockings yesterday.
17. I'm looking for *my briefcase* and *my books*.
18. The thief got into the house *through a basement window*.
19. *Those young boys* broke Mr. Flynn's front window.
20. Mr. Davis goes to Montreal *two or three times a year*.
21. The Slaters' daughter looks like *her grandmother*.
22. Charles got into trouble *because he didn't follow instructions*.
23. The meaning of that word is *"sad" or "unhappy."*
24. Mr. Smith put the reports *on Mr. Johnson's desk*.
25. The Taylors painted their house *blue and white*.
26. Charles asked his father and mother for *some money*.
27. That student has *a very poor* attitude toward his studies.
28. Miss Peters addressed the letter *to the A. B. C. Company*.
29. It's about *four hundred miles* to Washington D.C.
30. The tunnel to Brooklyn is *near the Battery Park*.
31. *Mr. Kaufman's car* is in the alley behind our house.
32. John's brother is going to study *at the University of Washington*.

HEARING AND SPEAKING LESSON 🔊

Listen carefully. Answer the questions with a full sentence.

1. *How many children do the Holts have?*
2. *Where did the accident happen?*
3.
4.
5.
6.
7.
8.
9.
10.
11.
12.
13.
14.
15.
16.
17.
18.
19.
20.
21.
22.
23.
24.
25.
26.
27.
28.
29.
30.
31.
32.

NEGATIVE QUESTIONS

Change these statements to simple negative questions. Make a contraction in each question. Study the two examples carefully.

1 He is in his office now. —*Isn't he in his office now?*
2 They studied the lesson. —*Didn't they study the lesson?*
3 Martha is going to go to the movies tonight.
4 Betty wore her new spring dress to the party.
5 There are some shelves in that closet.
6 The students knew the answers to the questions.
7 Mr. Anderson never drinks coffee in the morning.
8 The Smiths will arrive in Los Angeles tomorrow.
9 There is some milk in the refrigerator.
10 Professor Moore walked to school this morning.
11 Mr. Johnson will be in his office this afternoon.
12 Mr. Berg understands the instructions in the book.
13 That girl does all of her homework carefully.
14 The vice-president was at the meeting last Thursday.

NEGATIVE QUESTIONS WITH WHY

Change these negatives to negative questions with *why*. Make a contraction in each question. Study the two examples carefully.

1 He wasn't in class yesterday. —*Why wasn't he in class yesterday?*
2 She didn't write that letter. —*Why didn't she write that letter?*
3 Mr. Foster and Mr. Green weren't at the meeting.
4 Mr. Smith didn't get to work on time this morning.
5 Mr. Meyer didn't go to the lecture with the other students.
6 His secretary wasn't in the office at that time.
7 The Browns aren't going to go to Europe this year.
8 The students didn't write the last two lessons.
9 Those boys didn't study their English assignment last night.
10 There won't be anyone in this office tomorrow.
11 George doesn't know the irregular verbs yet.
12 Frank and John didn't do their share of the work.
13 That fellow didn't tell me about his suggestion until today.
14 Your paper wasn't on my desk before class this morning.

HEARING AND SPEAKING LESSON 91

Listen carefully. Answer the questions with a full sentence.

1. *Isn't he in his office now?*
2. *Didn't they study the lesson?*
3.
4.
5.
6.
7.
8.
9.
10.
11.
12.
13.
14.

HEARING AND SPEAKING LESSON 92

Listen carefully. Answer the questions with a full sentence.

1. *Why wasn't he in class yesterday?*
2. *Why didn't she write that letter?*
3.
4.
5.
6.
7.
8.
9.
10.
11.
12.
13.
14.

FREE WRITING PRACTICE(12)

What can you see in this picture?

I can see a policeman.

What is he doing now?

he is looking around the street.

What does the policeman do?

if a man breaks the law, the policeman arrests him and take the man to court.

FREE WRITING PRACTICE(13)

What can we do in the saving bank?

we put our money in the bank to save it. The bank uses our money and pays us for it. some banks pay us more than other banks. if I have money which I do not want to use now, I will put it in the bank. the bank will pay me for using my money. of course, the bank will pay me my money when I want it.

THE PERFECT PRESENT TENSE (1)

Write the correct form of the verb in parentheses in each sentence. Use only the perfect present tense. Study the examples carefully.

1. We (*visit*) that museum. —<u>We have visited that museum.</u>
2. Bill (*finish*) the work. —<u>Bill has finished the work.</u>
3. I (*travel, never*) by air. —<u>I have never traveled by air.</u>
4. Mr. Moore (*explain*) those two lessons to us already.
5. I (*live*) in this city almost all of my life.
6. That company (*hire*) twenty new workers since June.
7. The boys (*mention, already*) that matter to Mr. Brown.
8. We (*follow*) the instructions in the book carefully so far.
9. Pierre's English (*improve*) a great deal since July.
10. Betty (*copy*) all of the new words into her notebook.
11. The men (*try*) that method several times already.
12. Mr. Smith (*travel, never*) across the Atlantic by plane.
13. The company (*increase*) its production by twenty percent.
14. Up to now, we (*study*) almost every lesson in this book.

THE PERFECT PRESENT TENSE (2)

Write the correct form of the verb in parentheses in each sentence. Use only the perfect tense. The verbs in these sentences are irregular verbs. Check your answers carefully with the list of irregular verbs in the appendix.

1. We (*see*) that movie. —<u>We have seen that movie.</u>
2. He (*have*) his lunch already. —<u>He has had his lunch already.</u>
3. I (*be, never*) there before. —<u>I have never been there before.</u>
4. Richard (*take*) three different courses in English.
5. Miss Peters (*fly*) in an airplane only two other times.
6. The two girls (*do, already*) the dinner dishes.
7. I'm sorry. I (*forget*) the name of that new song.
8. Mr. and Mrs. Garcia (*be*) in this city for six months.
9. We (*know*) Mr. and Mrs. Smith for over twelve years.
10. I (*fall*) on these steep steps several times this week.
11. I think Mr. Harris (*have, already*) his lunch.
12. I (*read, already*) his letter and (*write*) a reply to him.
13. Carol and Martha (*have*) lots of practice in English so far.
14. We (*see, already*) Mr. Duncan and (*speak*) to him about that.

HEARING AND SPEAKING LESSON 🔊 93

Listen carefully. Answer the questions with a full sentence.

1. *We have visited that museum.*
2. *Bill has finished that work.*
3. *I have never traveled by air.*
4.
5.
6.
7.
8.
9.
10.
11.
12.
13.
14.

HEARING AND SPEAKING LESSON 🔊 94

Listen carefully. Answer the questions with a full sentence.

1. *We have seen that movie.*
2. *He has had his lunch already.*
3. *I have never been there before.*
4.
5.
6.
7.
8.
9.
10.
11.
12.
13.
14.

ASKING QUESTIONS

Change these statements to simple questions. Study the examples carefully.

1. Mr. Green has quit his job. —*Has Mr. Green quit his job?*
2. We have already done that lesson. —*Have we already done that lesson?*
3. John has already given his homework to Mr. Harris.
4. Mr. and Mrs. Burke have heard the good news.
5. Betty has copied all of the new words from the blackboard.
6. The students have already studied that lesson.
7. Your English has improved very much since September.
8. Those men have done their share of the work.
9. The director has mentioned his plan to the committee.
10. The weather has been very bad this past week.
11. Mr. and Mrs. Slater have taken good care of their car.
12. We have heard that radio program several times.
13. My friend Tom has always enjoyed that kind of work.
14. There have been some bad storms in this area recently.

MAKING NEGATIVES

Change these statements to negatives. Study the examples carefully.

1. We have seen that movie. —*We haven't seen that movie.*
2. Frank has taken that course. —*Frank hasn't taken that course.*
3. The students have written the last two lessons.
4. Miss Peters has finished those letters for Mr. Johnson.
5. Mr. Harris and Mr. Moore have eaten lunch.
6. That student has had much practice in conversation.
7. Mr. Moore has explained that part of the lesson.
8. Our friends have decided on a name for their baby.
9. My boss has hired some new workers in the past week.
10. We have discussed that part of the lesson very thoroughly.
11. Mr. Benson and his wife have been here since last August.
12. Tom's sister has told her parents about her plan.
13. There have been some bad storms in this area recently.
14. We've repaired the hole in the roof of our house.
15. Mr. Smith has said something to Mr. Fox about that problem.

HEARING AND SPEAKING LESSON

Listen carefully. Answer the questions with a full sentence.

1. *Has Mr. Green quit his job?*
2. *Have we already done that lesson?*
3. *Has John already given his homework to Mr. Harris?*
4.
5.
6.
7.
8.
9.
10.
11.
12.
13.
14.

HEARING AND SPEAKING LESSON

Listen carefully. Answer the questions with a full sentence.

1. *We haven't seen that movie.*
2. *Frank hasn't taken that course.*
3. *The students haven't written the last two lessons.*
4.
5.
6.
7.
8.
9.
10.
11.
12.
13.
14.
15.

REVIEW : TENSE FORMS

Change the verbs in these sentences (a) to the past tense, (b) to the future tense, and (c) to the perfect present tense. Study the examples carefully.

1. I spend my money. (a) *I spent my money.*
   (b) *I will spend my money.*
   (c) *I have spent my money.*

2. They use that one.
3. We study English together.
4. They discuss their work.
5. They have enough time.
6. I do all of the lessons.
7. He sits in that row.
8. I drive my car.
9. She hides her money.
10. We go to school.
11. He takes much time.

12. Does he eat there? (a) *Did he eat there?*
    (b) *Will he eat there?*
    (c) *Has he eaten there?*

13. Do you enjoy that work?
14. Does he write many letters?
15. Do you send many letters?
16. Do they explain everything?
17. Does she attend that class?
18. Do you have enough time?
19. Do they copy the sentences?
20. Does she have much trouble?
21. Does she do good work?
22. Do the students practice?

23. I don't stay there. (a) *I didn't stay there.*
    (b) *I won't stay there.*
    (c) *I haven't stayed there.*

24. He doesn't work hard.
25. I don't have any energy.
26. He doesn't pay his bills.
27. We don't see that fellow.
28. She doesn't use this one.
29. They don't remember it.
30. I don't do much work here.
31. He doesn't listen carefully.

HEARING AND SPEAKING LESSON

Listen carefully. Answer the questions with a full sentence.

1. (a)I spent my money. (b)I will spend my money. (c)I have spent my money.
2. (a)They used that one. (b)They will use that one. (c)They have used that one.
3.
4.
5.
6.
7.
8.
9.
10.
11.
12.
13. (a)Did you enjoy that work? (b)Will you enjoy that work? (c)Have you enjoyed that work?
14.
15.
16.
17.
18.
19.
20.
21.
22.
23.
24. (a)He didn't work hard. (b)He won't wok hard. (c)He hasn't work hard.
25.
26.
27.
28.
29.
30.
31.

USING IRREGULAR VERBS

Write the correct form of the verb in parentheses in each sentence. Use only the perfect present tense. Check your answers with the list of irregular verbs in the appendix.

1. Mr. Harris (*teach*) English at this school for five years.
2. I (*write*) three or four letters to that company.
3. The students in this class (*do*) those two lessons already.
4. I (*know*) Professor Moore for more than twelve years.
5. Richard (*take*) three courses in English at this school.
6. These steps are dangerous. I (*fall*) on them several times.
7. Mr. Kramer (*be*) in the United States for three years.
8. The janitor (*shut, already*) the back door.
9. The students (*read*) all of the stories in that book.
10. Marjorie (*choose*) a pretty dress for the party.
11. I (*speak*) to my boss about the problem several times.
12. That tree (*grow*) at least five feet since last year.
13. Miss King (*spend*) over eighteen hundred dollars since May.
14. Mr. and Mrs. Smith (*buy*) a new house in North Plains.
15. The real estate agent (*sell*) the Smith's old house.
16. Charles (*have*) a bad cold for a whole week.
17. I'm sorry. I (*forget*) the name of that book.
18. We (*hear, already*) that new song several times.
19. Mr. Wilson isn't here. He (*go*) out of town for the weekend.
20. Mr. Kennedy (*wear*) his blue suit to the office only twice.
21. I (*sit*) in this same seat since the first day of classes.
22. The money isn't in this drawer. Someone (*steal*) it!
23. Up to now, I (*understand*) every lesson in the book.
24. We (*have*) absolutely no trouble with our car so far.
25. No one (*find*) that girl's purse and gloves yet.
26. The weather (*be*) very warm ever since last Thursday.
27. Mr. Anderson and Mr. Brown (*have*) lunch already.
28. I (*see*) the Empire State Building hundreds of times.
29. We (*speak, already*) to the director and (*give*) him the message.
30. Grandmother (*fly, never*) in an airplane before.
31. You (*tear*) your shirt! There's a hole in the left sleeve.
32. I (*read, already*) the customer's letter and (*write*) a reply to him.

HEARING AND SPEAKING LESSON

Listen carefully. Answer the questions with a full sentence.

1. *Mr. Harris has taught English at this school for five years.*
2. *I have written three or four letters to that company.*

PERFECT PRESENT vs SIMPLE PAST

Write the correct form of the verb in parentheses in each sentence. Choose only the simple past tense (examples: *I worked, he took*) or the perfect present tense (examples: *I have worked, he has taken*). Notice the two examples.

1. I (*see*) that movie already. —*I have seen that movie already.*
2. I (*see*) that movie yesterday. —*I saw that movie yesterday.*
3. I (*read*) that novel by Faulkner several times before.
4. I (*read*) that novel again during my last vacation.
5. Mr. Foster (*study*) Spanish at New York University last year.
6. Mr. Foster (*study*) French in this class since last September.
7. Miss Cunningham (*live*) in Detroit from 1940 to 1946.
8. Miss Cunningham (*live*) in New York since that time.
9. Our guests (*have*) a good time at the party last night.
10. Our guests (*have*) a good time ever since their arrival.
11. Dr. and Mrs. Duncan (*see*) the Coliseum in Rome in 1948.
12. Dr. Duncan (*see*) the Statue of Liberty hundreds of times.
13. The Browns (*be*) in Detroit twice since Christmas.
14. The Browns (*be*) in San Francisco the week before last.
15. My wife and I (*travel*) by air many times in the past.
16. My wife and I (*travel*) to Mexico by air last summer.
17. The students (*finish, finally*) that hard exercise!
18. The students (*start*) that exercise about three hours ago.
19. We (*receive*) the boy's telegram at 8:00 p.m. last night.
20. We (*send, already*) them a special delivery reply.
21. Mr. and Mrs. Hanson (*visit*) Paris before the last war.
22. Mr. and Mrs. Hanson (*visit*) Paris many times since the war.
23. We (*study*) almost every lesson in this book so far.
24. We (*study*) a very hard lesson the day before yesterday.
25. I (*have*) a little trouble with my car last week.
26. However, I (*have*) no trouble with my car since then.
27. We (*watch, never*) that television program.
28. We (*watch*) an interesting program on television last night.
29. That tall fellow (*work*) here for the past three weeks.
30. Formerly, he (*work*) for the A.B.C. Company in Boston.
31. Mr. Shaw is my English teacher. He (*teach*) here for six years.
32. He (*finish*) his Ph. D. at Yale University seven years ago.

HEARING AND SPEAKING LESSON

Listen carefully. Answer the questions with a full sentence.

1. *I have seen that movie already. I have already seen that movie.*
2. *I saw that movie yesterday.*
3. *I have read that novel by Faulkner several times before.*
4. *I read that novel again during my last vacation.*

THE PRESENT TENSES

Use the correct form of the verb in parentheses in each sentence. Choose only the simple present tense (example : *he writes*), the continuous present tense(example : *he is writing*), or the perfect present tense (example : *he has written*).

1. We (*study*) English in this class since last September.
2. My teacher (*teach*) English at this school for six years.
3. Listen! I (*think*) someone (*knock*) at the front door.
4. Mr. Smith (*pay*) all of his bills at the end of the month.
5. I (*see*) the famous Grand Canyon in Arizona several times.
6. It (*rain, usually*) very much in that part of the United States.
7. Mr. and Mrs. Garcia (*be*) in New York for two months.
8. Those students (*make*) much progress since October.
9. My friend Frank (*owe*) Fred Foster fifty-five dollars.
10. I (*be*) sorry. I (*forget*) that fellow's name already.
11. Mr. Johnson's secretary (*sit*) at a different desk today.
12. I (*have*) no trouble with my English lessons up to now.
13. Richard (*look*) forward to his vacation next June.
14. The tall girl in the front seat (*come*) from South America.
15. Yes, we (*hear*) that new song several times already.
16. My wife and I (*live*) in this city for almost nine years.
17. The boys (*study*) their lessons together every afternoon.
18. Thomas (*have*) a good time here ever since his arrival.
19. I (*need*) some more money for my books and tuition.
20. At present, that author (*write*) a historical novel.
21. Our present teacher (*live*) in this city all of his life.
22. Miss Fox (*talk*) to someone on the telephone at the moment.
23. My friend Felix (*be*) in this country for a long time.
24. Up to the present, George (*do*) good work in this class.
25. Those four people (*be*) here since eight o'clock.
26. Daniel Soto (*work*) thirty-eight hours a week.
27. We (*write*) almost every exercise in this book up to now.
28. The weather (*get, generally*) quite hot in July and August.
29. So far, you (*make*) no mistakes on this exercise.
30. At the moment, I (*read*) a book about Alexander the Great.
31. Mr. Kent (*have*) that job in Pasadena since June first.

HEARING AND SPEAKING LESSON

Listen carefully. Answer the questions with a full sentence.

1. We have studied English in this class since last September.
2. My teacher is teaching English at this school for six years.
3. Listen! I think someone is knocking at the front door.
4. Mr. Smith pays all of his bills at the end of the month.

ANSWER PRESUMING QUESTIONS — 101

Complete these answer presuming questions. Also give the expected short answer to each question. Study the examples very carefully.

	QUESTION	ANSWER
1	The sun *is* shining now, *isn't it*?	Yes, it is.
2	Mr. Wilson *lives* there, *doesn't he*?	Yes, he does.
3	The men *haven't* done it yet, *have they*?	No, they haven't.
4	Mrs. Fox *didn't* speak to you, *did she*?	No, she didn't.
5	That *is* Mr. Kennedy's car, *isn't it*?	Yes, it is.
6	There *wasn't* anyone in the room, *was there*?	No, there wasn't.
7	Miss Peters wasn't in the office, ----?	----, ----.
8	Mr. Moore speaks French very well, ----?	----, ----.
9	Your friend didn't see you yesterday, ----?	----, ----.
10	Betty has written the letter already, ----?	----, ----.
11	They will be at your house tonight, ----?	----, ----.
12	There were some keys on the desk, ----?	----, ----.
13	Miss Kent doesn't have a car, ----?	----, ----.
14	Your guests had a very good time, ----?	----, ----.
15	The Browns aren't eating right now, ----?	----, ----.
16	The workers haven't done that yet, ----?	----, ----.
17	That isn't Mr. Johnson's briefcase, ----?	----, ----.
18	That bus goes to Washington Square, ----?	----, ----.
19	You have already seen that movie, ----?	----, ----.
20	Mary didn't leave the front door open, ----?	----, ----.
21	Mr. Green went home very late, ----?	----, ----.
22	Bill is studying at Columbia University, ----?	----, ----.
23	These aren't your cigarettes, ----?	----, ----.
24	Ed's brother finished school last year, ----?	----, ----.
25	There will be enough coffee for everyone, ----?	----, ----.
26	That last lesson wasn't very difficult, ----?	----, ----.
27	You study each vocabulary list carefully, ----?	----, ----.
28	The students did their work together, ----?	----, ----.
29	Bill had enough money for his books, ----?	----, ----.
30	The students haven't done that lesson, ----?	----, ----.

HEARING AND SPEAKING LESSON

Listen carefully. Answer the questions with a full sentence.

	QUESTION	ANSWER
1	The sun is shining now, isn't it?	Yes, it is.
2		
3		
4		
5		
6		
7	Miss Peters wasn't in the office, was she?	No, she wasn't.
8	Mr. Moore speaks French very well, Doesn't he?	Yes, he does.
9		
10		
11		
12		
13		
14		
15		
16		
17		
18		
19	You have already seen that movie, haven't you?	Yes, I have.
20		
21		
22		
23		
24		
25		
26		
27		
28		
29		
30		

FREE WRITING PRACTICE(14)

Listen to the song.

Forty-Niners

Oh my darling Clementine

in a cavern, in a canyon
excavating for a mine
dwelt a miner forty niner
and his daughter Clementine

*

oh my darling oh my darling
oh my darling Clementine
thou are lost and gone forever
dreadful sorry Clementine

*

light she was and like a fairy
and her shoes were number nine
herring boxes without topses
sandals were for Clementine

*

drove she ducklings to the water
every morning just at nine
hit her foot against a splinter
fell into the foaming brine

*

ruby lips above the water
blowing bubbles soft and fine
but alas I was no swimmer
so I lost my Clementine

*

how I missed her how I missed her
how I missed my Clementine
but I kissed her little sister
I forgot my Clementine

*

FREE WRITING PRACTICE(15)

in a cavern, in a canyon
excavating for a mine
dwelt a miner forty niner
and his daughter Clementine

oh my darling oh my darling
oh my darling Clementine
thou are lost and gone forever
dreadful sorry Clementine

light she was and like a fairy
and her shoes were number nine
herring boxes without topses
sandals were for Clementine

drove she ducklings to the water
every morning just at nine
hit her foot against a splinter
fell into the foaming brine

ruby lips above the water
blowing bubbles soft and fine
but alas I was no swimmer
so I lost my Clementine

SPECIAL EXPRESSIONS OF TIME   102

Choose *before, after, from,* or *ago* for the blank space in each sentence.

1. Our friends will arrive in this city a week ---- now.
2. Mr. Benson was here the week ---- last.
3. The men are leaving for Cuba the month ---- next.
4. Fred's brother finished school several years ----.
5. Bill and I went to that meeting the night ---- last.
6. Pierre will return to this country two years ---- now.
7. Our school year ended the month ---- last.
8. Mr. and Mrs. Fox left here two weeks ---- yesterday.
9. I'm going to go back to school the week ---- next.
10. Did you speak to Miss Davis the day ---- yesterday?
11. My friends will arrive here a week ---- next Sunday.
12. Mr. and Mrs. Taylor will get back the day ---- tomorrow.
13. I am leaving for South America a week ---- tomorrow.
14. I'll get back to the United States a month ---- now.
15. My friends left for Venezuela a week ---- yesterday.

EXPRESSIONS OF TIME(1)   103

Choose *in, on* or *at* for the blank space in each sentence.

1. The mailman delivered the letter ---- 1:45 p.m.
2. I woke up ---- three o'clock ---- the morning.
3. The weather is pleasant here ---- the spring.
4. Mr. Johnson's birthday is ---- February 20.
5. We saw Smith in Los Angeles ---- September.
6. Mr. and Mrs. Brown are leaving for England ---- Saturday.
7. The flight from Miami arrived in New York ---- noon.
8. Mr. Anderson plans to return to California ---- the third of April.
9. Mr. Shaw graduated from the university ---- 1949.
10. My English class starts ---- ten minutes after three.
11. Mr. Foster will get back from Chicago ---- the tenth of January.
12. Many people take their vacations ---- June, July, and August.
13. Are you going to study ---- the afternoon or ---- night?
14. We had a wonderful time at that party ---- Friday night.

HEARING AND SPEAKING LESSON 102

Listen carefully. Answer the questions with a full sentence.

1. *Our Friends will arrive in this city a week from now.*
2. *Mr. Benson was here the week before next.*
3.
4.
5.
6.
7.
8.
9.
10.
11.
12.
13.
14.
15.

HEARING AND SPEAKING LESSON 103

Listen carefully. Answer the questions with a full sentence.

1. *The mailman delivered the letter at 1:45 p.m.*
2. *I woke up at three o'clock in the morning.*
3.
4.
5.
6.
7.
8.
9.
10.
11.
12.
13.
14.

EXPRESSIONS OF TIME (2) — 104

Choose *in*, *on*, or *at* for the blank space in each sentence.

1. This English class seemed very easy ---- first.
2. ---- present, we are studying the use of prepositions.
3. Did you get to work ---- time yesterday morning?
4. Did you get to the meeting ---- time for the movie?
5. Both of us were in San Francisco ---- that time.
6. ---- the future, please write the exercises more carefully.
7. I see a musical comedy on Broadway once ---- a while.
8. ---- the beginning, the work seemed very difficult to me.
9. My friend came back with the money ---- no time ---- all.
10. From now ----, please study ---- least two hours a day.
11. We went out for coffee ---- the middle of the afternoon.
12. I've mentioned it to him ---- several different occasions.
13. You're making too much noise. Stop that ---- once!
14. Why don't you call him? I'll wait here ---- the meantime.

REVIEW : EXPRESSIONS OF TIME — 105

Choose *in*, *on*, or *at* for the blank space in each sentence.

1. My wife and I will return to New York ---- the fifth of August.
2. Mr. Kramer and his family came to this country ---- 1950.
3. He had a lot of trouble with English ---- the beginning.
4. ---- present, we are using a different English book.
5. Our visitors are going to go to that museum ---- Thursday.
6. Our English teacher closes the door ---- ten minutes after two.
7. Do you usually get to work ---- time ---- the morning?
8. The weather generally gets quite hot ---- July and August.
9. We plan to leave for Europe early ---- the spring.
10. The students finished those two exercises ---- no time ---- all.
11. Our baby was born ---- two o'clock ---- the afternoon May 2.
12. Please get ready now. ---- the meantime, I'll call our friends.
13. This English book seemed very easy to me ---- first.
14. Our friends are going to visit us here ---- Sunday night.
15. Well, I've finished this terrible exercise ---- last!

HEARING AND SPEAKING LESSON 104

Listen carefully. Answer the questions with a full sentence.

1. *This English class seemed very easy at first.*
2. *At present, we are studying the use of prepositions.*
3.
4.
5.
6.
7.
8.
9.
10.
11.
12.
13.
14.

HEARING AND SPEAKING LESSON 105

Listen carefully. Answer the questions with a full sentence.

1. *My wife and I will return to New York on the fifth of August.*
2.
3. *He had a lot of trouble with English in the beginning.*
4.
5.
6.
7.
8.
9.
10.
11.
12.
13.
14.
15.

EXPRESSIONS OF TIME(3)

In each section, choose one of the two indicated words for each sentence.

SINCE vs FOR

1. Mr. Berg has studied English in this class ---- eight months.
2. My friend has studied English in this class ---- last October.
3. The Browns have lived in this city ---- 1948.
4. The Wilsons have lived in New York ---- six years.
5. Mr. Smith worked for the Ajax Company ---- one year.
6. Mr. Smith has worked for our company ---- that time.
7. Alice has been here ---- the beginning of the year.
8. Her sister has been in San Francisco ---- a long time.

SINCE vs IN

1. Mr. and Mrs. Hanson lived in Chicago ---- 1947.
2. Mr. and Mrs. Hanson have lived in this city ---- 1948.
3. We haven't seen our friends the Flynns ---- August.
4. Mr. and Mrs. Flynn left for South America ---- August.
5. Frank's parents returned from Canada ---- the fall.
6. Frank's parents have lived in their new apartment ---- last fall.
7. Mr. Johnson hasn't had any free time ---- this morning.
8. Mr. Johnson had several important meetings ---- the morning.

FOR vs IN

1. Mr. Smith worked for the Container Corporation ---- 1951.
2. Mr. Smith worked for the corporation ---- one year.
3. My wife and I usually take our vacation ---- the summer.
4. We usually stay in Vermont or Maine ---- a whole month.
5. Professor Moore came to this university ---- 1939.
6. Professor Moore has taught here ---- seventeen years.
7. Fred's sister has had her diploma ---- over six weeks now.
8. She received her diploma from Michigan State University ---- June.

HEARING AND SPEAKING LESSON

Listen carefully. Answer the questions with a full sentence.

SINCE vs FOR

1. Mr. Berg has studied English in this class for eight months.
2. My friend has studied English in this class since last October.
3.
4.
5.
6.
7.
8.

SINCE vs IN

1. Mr. and Mrs. Hanson lived in Chicago in 1947.
2. Mr. and Mrs. Hanson have lived in this city since 1948.
3.
4.
5.
6.
7.
8.

FOR vs IN

1. Mr Smith worked for the Container Corporation in 1951.
2. Mr. Smith worked for the corporation for one year.
3.
4.
5.
6.
7.
8.

EXPRESSIONS OF TIME(4)

In each section, choose one of the two indicated words for each sentence.

BY vs IN

1. Thomas and Richard will be there ---- ten o'clock.
2. My friends will be there ---- two or three hours.
3. Will you finish the work ---- September 10?
4. I'll finish all of the work ---- three months.
5. I'll lend you my dictionary ---- a day or two.
6. Don't bother, I'll have my own dictionary ---- then.
7. We'll go there at six-thirty. ---- that time, Tom will be there.
8. I'm sure you will not finish the work ---- that amount of time.

BY vs UNTIL

1. Bill is there now. He'll be there ---- ten o'clock.
2. Bill isn't there now. But he'll be there ---- ten o'clock.
3. Don't hurry. The train won't leave ---- 5:45 p.m.
4. We'll certainly get to the station ---- 5:45 p.m.
5. Please return in an hour. I'll be ready ---- then.
6. I'll be back very soon. Wait right here ---- then.
7. Our guests stayed here ---- twelve o'clock last night.
8. ---- twelve o'clock, we were practically asleep in our chairs.

BY vs FOR

1. We'll have that report ready for you ---- 4:00 p.m.
2. We'll work on that report ---- the next two hours.
3. I'm leaving now, but I'll be back here noon.
4. I'll be away from my office ---- several hours today.
5. The highway department will finish that road ---- 1962.
6. The construction company has already worked on it ---- one year.
7. Please don't tell my friends the news ---- a few days.
8. Why not? Your friends will know all about it ---- that time.

HEARING AND SPEAKING LESSON

Listen carefully. Answer the questions with a full sentence.

BY vs IN

1. *Thomas and Richard will be there by ten o'clock.*
2. *My friends will be there in two or three hours.*
3.
4.
5.
6.
7.
8.

BY vs UNTIL

1. *Bill is there now. He'll be there until ten o'clock.*
2. *Bill isn't there now. But he'll be there by ten o'clock.*
3.
4.
5.
6.
7.
8.

BY vs FOR

1. *We'll have that report ready for you by 4:00 p.m.*
2. *We'll work on that report for the next two hours.*
3.
4.
5.
6.
7.
8.

EXPRESSIONS OF TIME (5)

In each section, choose one of the two indicated words for each sentence.

UNTIL vs FOR

1. I waited for you right there ---- five o'clock.
2. I waited for you right there ---- an hour and a half.
3. Mr. and Mrs. Carson will be in London ---- September.
4. The Carsons are going to stay in London ---- two months.
5. Our guests will remain with us ---- one more day.
6. They are going to stay here ---- the day after tomorrow.
7. Mr. Wilson won't be away from the office ---- very long.
8. Why don't you wait here in the office ---- then?

UNTIL vs IN

1. The train will leave the station ---- ten minutes.
2. The train won't leave the station ---- 2:30 p.m.
3. Mr. Burke will be back here ---- nine or ten days.
4. Mr. Burke will stay in San Diego ---- a week from Friday.
5. You will probably finish all of the work ---- an hour.
6. However, you will probably be very busy with it ---- that time.
7. Miss Stewart will be ready to leave ---- a little while.
8. Miss Stewart won't be ready to leave ---- eight o'clock.

FOR vs IN

1. The train to Chicago will leave ---- five minutes.
2. The train will stay in the station ---- five minutes more.
3. Are your friends going to be in Wisconsin ---- a long time?
4. No, they'll be back in this city ---- a week or two.
5. We usually go from Detroit to New York ---- three hours.
6. My brother and his wife lived in Detroit ---- three years.
7. Are you leaving now? No, I'll leave ---- a little while.
8. Are you leaving now? Yes, I'll be away ---- a little while.

HEARING AND SPEAKING LESSON 🔊

Listen carefully. Answer the questions with a full sentence.

UNTIL vs FOR

1. *I waited for you right there until five o'clock.*
2. *I waited for you right there for an hour and a half.*
3.
4.
5.
6.
7.
8.

UNTIL vs IN

1. *The train will leave the station in ten minutes.*
2. *The train won't leave the station until 2:30 p.m.*
3.
4.
5.
6.
7.
8.

FOR vs IN

1. *The train to Chicago will leave in five minutes.*
2. *The train will stay in the station for five minutes more.*
3.
4.
5.
6.
7.
8.

REVIEW : EXPRESSIONS OF TIME

Choose *for, until, by* or *in* for the blank space in each sentence.

1. I'm going to stay there ---- a year and a half.
2. I'll complete all of the work ---- noon tomorrow.
3. The man waited ---- eight o'clock. Then he left.
4. Will you get back from Newark ---- tomorrow night?
5. He's not here now, but he'll be back ---- a little while.
6. Mr. and Mrs. Kirby lived in Oregon ---- three years.
7. ---- this time, the Smiths have already arrived in Miami.
8. Are they going to remain in Florida ---- a long time?
9. They're going to return to New York late ---- the spring.
10. I worked on my assignment ---- eleven o'clock last night.
11. Mr. Berovski first came to this country ---- 1949.
12. The entire office staff worked ---- six thirty last night.
13. I'm going to stop ---- a few minutes and take a rest.
14. Our friends will stay in Europe ---- April or May.

REVIEW : EXPRESSIONS OF TIME

Choose *for, until, since*, or *at* for the blank space in each sentence.

1. The report won't be ready for us ---- noon tomorrow.
2. Everything will be ready for you ---- 12:00 p.m. sharp.
3. I've been in this class ---- the beginning of the semester.
4. ---- that time, everything seemed very easy to me.
5. My friends Roger and Dick were in Chicago ---- four months.
6. Frank won't get back here ---- later this afternoon.
7. He'll probably get back to the office ---- four or four-thirty.
8. Mr. and Mrs. Bianca lived in Naples, Italy ---- 1940.
9. Then they moved to Sao Paulo, Brazil ---- a year or two.
10. Mr. and Mrs. Bianca have lived in New York ---- 1947.
11. They are going to stay in New York ---- 1960.
12. Bill hasn't mentioned that matter ---- the last election.
13. He probably won't say anything about it ---- the next election.
14. ---- two days ago, practically everyone agreed with you.
15. ---- that time, everyone has changed his mind about it.

HEARING AND SPEAKING LESSON 🔊   109

Listen carefully. Answer the questions with a full sentence.

1. *I'm going to stay here for a year and a half.*
2. *I'll complete all of the work by noon tomorrow.*
3.
4.
5.
6.
7.
8.
9.
10.
11.
12.
13.
14.

HEARING AND SPEAKING LESSON 🔊   110

Listen carefully. Answer the questions with a full sentence.

1. *The report won't be ready for us until noon tomorrow.*
2. *Everything will be ready for you by 12:00 p.m. sharp.*
3.
4.
5.
6.
7.
8.
9.
10.
11.
12.
13.
14.
15.

FREE WRITING PRACTICE(16)

James Johnson is my name. I work in the main office of a big company. Twenty people work in that office every day. Mr. Wilson is my boss. He works very hard. Almost everyone works hard. Of course, a few people don't work hard.

Mr. Wilson has a private office. He also has a secretary. Miss Stewart is his secretary. She helps Mr. Wilson. She doesn't help me. I don't have a private office. But I have my own secretary. My secretary is Mary Peters.

Mr. Wilson meets all of the important visitors. I don't meet visitors. Miss Stewart doesn't meet visitors either. Mr. Wilson talks to visitors. I occasionally talk to visitors too. But I don't usually talk to visitors.

Mr. Wilson writes many letters every day. He sends many letters to customers. I write letters too. I send letters to other companies. But I don't send letters to customers.

I often study statistics. Then I write reports for Mr. Wilson. He studies the reports carefully. I get the statistics from my assistants. I have two assistants, Smith and Green. They help me very much. They don't write letters. They collect information from other people. Then they give the information to my secretary. She collects information from other people too. Then she gives the information to me.

My secretary doesn't write reports. But she write many letters for me. She also opens my mail. She reads the mail carefully. She gives me the important letters. She doesn't give me the other letters. I read the important letters too. Then I answer the letters. My secretary answers the other letters.

FREE WRITING PRACTICE(17)

James Johnson is my name. I work in the main office of a big company.

"A BRIEF HISTORY OF A.F. ROSSI"

Select the correct preposition for each blank space. Use only the prepositions *since, for, ago, in, on, at.*

A. F. Rossi

Mr. Rossi was born ---- Genoa, Italy ---- the year 1957. He was born ---- Tuesday, March 15, ---- midnight. He lived ---- Genoa ---- eight years. Then he moved to Rome ---- 1965. He fell in love with that city ---- that time. He has written a lot of stories about Rome ---- that time. However, it has been quite a long time ---- his last year ---- that city. He went to school ---- Rome ---- eight years. He quit school there ---- June, 1973. ---- July 15, he left ---- Switzerland. He arrived ---- Lausanne late ---- night two days later. He went to a private school ---- that city ---- two years. Today, he often speaks about the wonderful time he had ---- that school many years ----. ---- the end of those two years, he left ---- France. ---- first, he felt very homesick. However, he finally got a job ---- the staff of a large newspaper. It was hard work ---- the beginning. He didn't have much experience ---- that time. That was ---- 1975. Of course, he has gained a great deal of experience ---- then. But ---- those days, he was only a beginner ---- that field. ---- the beginning of the next year, he got a job ---- a publishing house. He worked ---- that concern ---- four years. Mr. Rossi came to the United States ---- the spring of 1980. He became a citizen ---- the twentieth of April, 1985. He has had a house ---- this city ---- that time. ---- all, he has lived ---- this country ---- quite a long time. Mr. Rossi took a course ---- English a number of years ----. He started his course ---- ten o'clock ---- the morning ---- October 7, 1983. He studied English ---- two years. Mr. Rossi has also studied German and Spanish ---- that time. He studied German ---- the summer of 1990, and he started his Spanish course ---- February, 1993. He studied that language ---- three years. Mr. Rossi went to South America six years ----, and he stayed there ---- two years. Then he returned to the United States ---- good. He has also written many things about South America ---- that trip. Mr. Rossi has been a professional writer ---- 1975. He wrote his first article ---- 1975. ---- then, he has written almost 800 articles and stories.

HEARING AND SPEAKING LESSON

REVIEW : VERB FORMS   112

Read the story about Mr. Rossi on page 184. Then write the correct form of the verb in each of the following sentences.

1. Mr. Rossi   (*be*) born in the year 1957.
2. Mr. Rossi   (*write*) almost eight hundred articles.
3. Mr. Rossi   (*come*) to the United States in the spring of 1980.
4. Mr. Rossi   (*live*) in the United States since 1980.
5. Mr. Rossi   (*study*) the German language in the year 1990.
6. Mr. Rossi   (*gain*) much experience since his first job.
7. Mr. Rossi   (*be, never*) in Canada or Alaska.
8. Mr. Rossi   (*leave*) Genoa, Italy after eight years.
9. Mr. Rossi   (*study*) two languages since the year 1990.
10. Mr. Rossi   (*take*) English courses from 1985 to 1987.
11. Mr. Rossi   (*live*) in the United States for a long time.
12. Mr. Rossi   (*study*) Spanish at a school for three years.
13. Mr. Rossi   (*have*) a house in the United States since 1982.
14. Mr. Rossi   (*be*) a professional writer since 1975.

REVIEW : QUESTION FORMS   113

Give a complete answer to each question about "A Brief History of A.F. Rossi."

1 When was Mr. Rossi born? 2 How long ago was he born? 3 How long did he live in Genoa? 4 When did he leave Genoa? 5 How long did he go to school in Rome? 6 When did he quit school in Rome? 7 When did he leave for Switzerland? 8 How long has he been in the United States? 9 How many years ago did he leave France? 10 When did he leave for South America? 11 How many years did he go to school in Lausanne? 12 When did he get his first job on the staff of a newspaper? 13 When did he finish his English course? 14 In what year did he finish his Spanish course? 15 How many languages does he know in all? 16 How many years ago did he get his job in the French publishing house? 17 In what year did he leave that job in the publishing house? 18 Where did Mr. Rossi go in 1975? 19 When did Mr. Rossi become a citizen of the United States? 20 How many years has he been a writer? 21 When did he return to the United States for good? 22 Where was Mr. Rossi five years ago? 23 What country is he going to visit next? 24 How many years ago did he write his first article?

HEARING AND SPEAKING LESSON 🔊 112

Listen carefully. Answer the questions with a full sentence.

1. *Mr. Rossi was born in the year 1957.*
2. *Mr. Rossi wrote almost eight hundred articles.*
3.
4.
5.
6.
7.
8.
9.
10.
11.
12.
13.
14.

HEARING AND SPEAKING LESSON 🔊 113

Listen carefully. Answer the questions with a full sentence.

1 *He was born in 1957.* **2** *He was born 56 years ago.* **3**
4 **5** **6**
7 **8**
9
10 **11**
12 **13**
14
15 **16**
17
18 **19**
20
21 **22**
23 **24**

EXPRESSIONS OF PLACE

Choose *in*, *on*, or *at* for the blank space in each sentence.

1. Mr. and Mrs. Kennedy live ---- West End Avenue.
2. Did you buy your new car ---- Detroit or here?
3. The Browns were ---- Greece and Italy two years ago.
4. Mr. Foster works ---- 667 E. 76th Street ---- New York.
5. The Johnson's garage is ---- back of their house.
6. Would you please park your car ---- the driveway.
7. Mr. and Mrs. Smith stayed ---- the Lincoln Hotel ---- Boston.
8. I'll meet you ---- the corner of 34th Street and Broadway.
9. How did you enjoy your vacation ---- Europe last year?
10. Alice isn't ---- home right now. She's ---- school.
11. There are national parks ---- every section of the country.
12. The Empire State Building is the tallest building ---- New York.
13. Do your friends live ---- Manhattan or ---- Long Island?
14. Mr. and Mrs. Johnson's house is ---- 420 East Boulevard.
15. Turn left ---- the corner. The house is ---- the left side.
16. Don't walk ---- the street! Walk here ---- the sidewalk.
17. Our friends are going to meet us ---- Times Square tonight.
18. Our friends arrived ---- New York the week before last.
19. Mr. Carson arrived ---- the airport half an hour early.
20. Have you and your wife ever traveled ---- a large ocean liner?
21. My friend and I always ride to school ---- the bus.
22. We usually study our English lessons ---- the way to school.
23. Please move over. You are standing ---- my way.
24. Mr. Johnson's office is ---- the sixth floor of the building.
25. Mrs. Roland is sitting ---- the desk ---- front of the door.
26. Listen! I think there is someone ---- the front door.
27. Are you and Frank ---- the same literature class?
28. Yes, ---- fact he and I sit together ---- the first row.
29. Did you put those two packages ---- the table ---- the hall?
30. No, I didn't. Did you look ---- the top drawer of your desk?
31. Someone probably put the packages ---- the shelf ---- the closet.
32. There's paper ---- the floor. Please put it ---- the wastebasket.

HEARING AND SPEAKING LESSON

Listen carefully. Answer the questions with a full sentence.

1. *Mr. and Mrs. Kennedy live on West End Avenue.*
2. *Did you buy your new car in Detroit or here?*

VERBS WITH ALLIED PREPOSITIONS

Select the correct preposition for the blank space in each sentence.

1. When do you plan to leave ---- South America?
2. Mr. Adams went ---- a walk ---- the park this afternoon.
3. Miss Peters is going to ask her boss ---- some advice.
4. Tom's friends are laughing ---- his funny answer.
5. Why don't you and Fred ever listen ---- classical music?
6. Don't worry ---- that matter. It's not very important.
7. Those books and papers belong ---- someone else.
8. We all looked ---- Dick's billfold. We finally found it.
9. How much did your friend pay ---- those theater tickets?
10. When do the Andersons expect to arrive ---- New York?
11. Mr. and Mrs. Anderson will arrive ---- the airport ---- 2:00 p.m.
12. Mr. Rossi is working ---- an article ---- a national magazine.
13. Mrs. Burke's brother borrowed some money ---- her.
14. Why did Mrs. Burke lend the money ---- her brother?
15. I don't want to argue ---- you ---- that matter ---- this time.
16. Our visitors complained ---- the bad weather ---- this region.
17. The company insisted ---- an immediate reply ---- their letter.
18. Martha's sister is shopping ---- a new spring hat today.
19. Frank always depends ---- his brother for assistance.
20. This English book consists ---- two separate sections.
21. Have Don and Dorothy decided ---- a name for their baby yet?
22. Mary reminded Mr. Fox ---- his appointment the next day.
23. Would you please substitute his name ---- mine ---- that list?
24. Mr. Perez is translating that book ---- Spanish ---- English.
25. Professor Moore glanced ---- his wrist watch quickly.
26. We introduced our guests ---- Mr. Johnson and Mr. Wilson.
27. All of the members objected ---- the chairman's suggestion.
28. The men will probably rely ---- you ---- some assistance.
29. That fellow constantly boasts ---- his influential friends.
30. I think you have confused that word ---- another one.
31. I hope the director will cooperate ---- us ---- that matter.
32. We don't want to interfere ---- our visitors' plans ---- any way.

HEARING AND SPEAKING LESSON

Listen carefully. Answer the questions with a full sentence.

1. When do you plan to leave for South America?
2. Mr. Adams went for a walk in the park this afternoon.
3. Miss Peters is going to ask her boss for some advice.
4.
5.
6.
7.
8.
9.
10.
11.
12.
13.
14.
15.
16.
17.
18.
19.
20.
21.
22.
23.
24.
25.
26.
27.
28.
29.
30.
31.
32.

ADJECTIVES WITH ALLIED PREPOSITIONS

Select the correct preposition for the blank space in each sentence.

1. Are you ready ---- the English examination?
2. My friend Roger is very excited ---- his new job.
3. Mr. and Mrs. Brown are proud ---- their new house.
4. Alice has been absent ---- the last two classes.
5. Why were those girls mad ---- Frank and you?
6. They were mad ---- our attitude ---- their suggestion.
7. John is more interested ---- history than English.
8. Please be careful ---- this tool. It's very delicate.
9. I am very sorry ---- my mistake. I wasn't careful enough.
10. Everyone feels very sorry ---- that poor old man.
11. All of the members were pleased ---- the final result.
12. We're not accustomed ---- this very cold weather yet.
13. Everyone ---- the group was very polite ---- our guests.
14. I'm angry ---- Richard Jones ---- a very good reason.
15. Mr. Berg wasn't very sure ---- the answers ---- his paper.
16. We have plenty ---- time. We'll get ---- school ---- time.
17. Daniel Soto and his wife are quite fond ---- strong coffee.
18. I hope you are prepared ---- a great deal ---- criticism.
19. I think that young girl is afraid ---- cats and dogs.
20. That author is famous ---- his novels ---- the Civil War.
21. That restaurant ---- Tenth Street is known ---- its fine food.
22. Those two pails are full ---- water ---- the rain last night.
23. The police are very suspicious ---- those two fellows.
24. I'm getting tired ---- that student's constant excuses.
25. Your example is similar ---- mine but different ---- Fred's.
26. That man's face seems very familiar ---- me.
27. Are you familiar ---- that peculiar American expression?
28. They are not aware ---- my strong feelings ---- that matter.
29. Tom and I are grateful ---- you ---- all of your assistance.
30. That kind of dress is not suitable ---- certain occasions.
31. Betty is always very considerate ---- other people's feelings.
32. The quality of this shirt is not equal ---- the quality of that one.

HEARING AND SPEAKING LESSON

Listen carefully. Answer the questions with a full sentence.

1. *Are you ready for the English examination?*
2. *My friend Roger is very exited about his new job.*
3. *Mr. and Mrs. Brown are proud of there new house.*

THE WORDS STILL AND ANY MORE 117

Choose *still* or *any more* for the blank space in each sentence. Observe the word order in these sentences carefully. Study the first four examples.

1. My friend William is *still* at the library.
2. Mr. Foster *still* plans to leave as soon as possible.
3. My wife and I *still* haven't found an apartment.
4. Professor Moore doesn't walk to school *any more.*
5. Mr. Johnson is ---- talking to his two assistants.
6. Doesn't Elizabeth's father smoke cigarettes ----?
7. Are the Hiltons ---- staying with their friends in Detroit?
8. Mr. Benson isn't the chairman of that committee ----?
9. Fred ----- doesn't agree with you and me on that point.
10. Are you fellows ---- worrying about the same problem?
11. Richard and I don't eat lunch at the cafeteria -----.
12. Mr. Green ----- hasn't spoken to Mr. Wilson about my plan.
13. Don and Dorothy Burke don't watch that television program ----.
14. Are Mr. Meyer and Mr. Berg ---- studying English at this school?

THE WORDS ALREADY AND YET 118

Choose *already* or *yet* for the blank space in each sentence. Observe the word order in these sentences carefully. Study the first three examples.

1. We have *already* spoken to the men about the problem.
2. Most of the guests have gone home *already.*
3. My friends haven't arrived from San Francisco *yet.*
4. Some of the students were ---- in the classroom.
5. We haven't started the advanced section of this book ----.
6. The Browns have ----- had their new car for two weeks.
7. Mr. Green has had no opportunity to mention it ----.
8. Most of the students have done those two lessons ----.
9. Not many people in this neighborhood have heard the news ----.
10. The students have learned a lot of things about English ----?
11. Have you seen the movie at the Paramount Theater ----?
12. My secretary has ----- written a reply to that inquiry.
13. Miss Peters is sitting at her desk ----, isn't she?
14. Those two students have done that work ----, haven't they?
15. Thomas and Richard haven't done their part of it ----, have they?

HEARING AND SPEAKING LESSON 117

Listen carefully. Answer the questions with a full sentence.

1 *My friend William is still at the library.*
2
3
4
5
6
7
8
9
10
11
12
13
14

HEARING AND SPEAKING LESSON 118

Listen carefully. Answer the questions with a full sentence.

1 *We have already spoken to the men about the problem.*
2
3 *My friends haven't arrived from San Francisco yet.*
4
5
6
7
8
9
10
11
12
13
14
15

REVIEW : STILL, ALREADY, AND YET   119

Choose *still, already,* or *yet* for the blank space in each sentence.

1. Tom and Fred have ---- done Exercises 119 and 120.
2. The other students haven't done those two exercises ----.
3. As a matter of fact, they're ---- doing Exercise 118.
4. Don't you know the meaning of that word ----?
5. I think your English vocabulary is ---- much too small.
6. Do you ---- do your assignments with your friend Edward?
7. You have ---- spoken to Mr. Johnson, haven't you?
8. No, I ---- haven't had a chance to speak to Mr. Johnson.
9. Does Mr. Johnson know anything about our problem ----?
10. Miss Peters is ---- Mr. Johnson's secretary, isn't she?
11. Has the company bought an electric typewriter for her ----?
12. That isn't necessary. Miss Peters has got one ----.
13. My wife and I ---- live in the same apartment house.
14. We ---- don't have enough money to buy a house in North Plains.
15. Haven't you and your wife saved enough money for a house ----?

THE WORDS ALSO, TOO, AND EITHER   120

Choose *also, too,* or *either* for the blank space in each sentence. In some cases, both *also* and *too* are possible. Study the first four examples.

1. I enjoy classical music. But I <u>*also*</u> enjoy popular music.
2. Richard is working now. Thomas is working now <u>*also.*</u>
3. Richard is working now. Thomas is working now <u>*too.*</u>
4. Alice didn't do that work. I didn't do that work <u>*either.*</u>

5. They watched television. We watched television ----.
6. Frank collects stamps. He ---- collects interesting coins.
7. Mr. Smith won't be at the meeting. I won't be there ----.
8. She has already seen that movie. I've seen that movie ----.
9. Dick plays tennis very well. He ---- plays golf very well.
10. I don't like American coffee, and I don't like hot dogs ----.
11. Betty's going to go in your car. I'm going to go with you ----.
12. I haven't had any free time. She hasn't had any free time ----.
13. I was in Europe last year. Were you in Europe last year ----?
14. I haven't finished the work yet. Haven't you finished ----?

HEARING AND SPEAKING LESSON 119

Listen carefully. Answer the questions with a full sentence.

1. *Tom and Fred have already done Exercise 119 and 120.*
2. *The other students haven't done those two exercises yet.*
3. *As a matter of fact, they'er still doing Exercise 118.*
4.
5.
6.
7.
8.
9.
10.
11.
12.
13.
14.
15.

HEARING AND SPEAKING LESSON 120

Listen carefully. Answer the questions with a full sentence.

1. *I enjoy classical music. But I also enjoy popular music.*
2.
3.
4.
5.
6.
7.
8.
9.
10.
11.
12.
13.
14.

FREE WRITING PRACTICE(18)

James Johnson is my name. I work in the main office of a big company. Twenty people work in that office every day. Mr. Wilson is my boss. He works very hard. Almost everyone works hard. Of course, a few people don't work hard.

Mr. Wilson has a private office. He also has a secretary. Miss Stewart is his secretary. She helps Mr. Wilson. She doesn't help me. I don't have a private office. But I have my own secretary. My secretary is Mary Peters.

Mr. Wilson meets all of the important visitors. I don't meet visitors. Miss Stewart doesn't meet visitors either. Mr. Wilson talks to visitors. I occasionally talk to visitors too. But I don't usually talk to visitors.

Mr. Wilson writes many letters every day. He sends many letters to customers. I write letters too. I send letters to other companies. But I don't send letters to customers.

I often study statistics. Then I write reports for Mr. Wilson. He studies the reports carefully. I get the statistics from my assistants. I have two assistants, Smith and Green. They help me very much. They don't write letters. They collect information from other people. Then they give the information to my secretary. She collects information from other people too. Then she gives the information to me.

My secretary doesn't write reports. But she write many letters for me. She also opens my mail. She reads the mail carefully. She gives me the important letters. She doesn't give me the other letters. I read the important letters too. Then I answer the letters. My secretary answers the other letters.

FREE WRITING PRACTICE(19)

James Johnson is my name.

USING CONTRACTIONS

Read each sentence aloud. If possible, use a contraction (for example: *she is - she's, they did not - they didn't, etc.*). In some sentences, there are two possibilities. Contractions are not possible in a few sentences.

1. He does not like it.
2. I am not a student.
3. She has seen it.
4. It will be ready for you.
5. She is not a teacher.
6. Where is the office?
7. I am very busy now.
8. They did not write it.
9. John was not absent.
10. When are you leaving?
11. They do not know that.
12. We are very unhappy.
13. It is very cold outside.
14. She was not late.
15. What is that?
16. There is a Salesman here.
17. That is a very big house.
18. It did not rain very hard.
19. Who will do that work?
20. We have finished it.
21. It was not very good.
22. She is not here now.
23. Those are ours.
24. He will help us soon.
25. They have been in Cuba.
26. Who are those people?
27. We are going to go soon.
28. I will not have any time.
29. It is not ready yet.
30. That was interesting.
31. That is a suitcase.
32. There is not a thing here.
33. They have not done it.
34. What is this?
35. He does not know it.
36. She is not ready yet.
37. Whose are those?
38. They were not angry.
39. You did not come.
40. You have not heard it.
41. There are books here.
42. I do not see it yet.
43. It was not difficult.
44. There is a man here.
45. They will not be here.
46. It did not rain hard.
47. Who is that fellow?
48. We have not been there.
49. That is very good.
50. I have eaten already.
51. There was a party there.
52. They are not going to go.
53. She is not very nervous.
54. It is very pretty.
55. That is very interesting.
56. I was not in the room.
57. I am ready now.
58. They were not here.

HEARING AND SPEAKING LESSON

Listen carefully. Answer the questions with a full sentence.

1. *He doesn't like it.*
2. *I'm not a student.*
3. *She's seen it.*
4.
5.
6.
7.
8.
9.
10.
11.
12.
13.
14.
15.
16.
17.
18.
19.
20.
21.
22.
23.
24.
25.
26.
27.
28.
29.
30.
31.
32.
33.
34.
35.
36.
37.
38.
39.
40.
41.
42.
43.
44.
45.
46.
47.
48.
49.
50.
51.
52.
53.
54.
55.
56.
57.
58.

WORD ORDER : FREQUENCY WORDS

Put each frequency word in the correct position in the following sentence. Study the first four examples carefully.

1. (*always*) That man is late. *That man is always late.*
2. (*usually*) Is it cold in the winter? *Is it usually cold in the winter?*
3. (*seldom*) He returns before 2:30. *He seldom returns before 2:30.*
4. (*never*) I have seen that statue. *I have never seen that statue.*
5. (*usually*) William and Richard work very hard.
6. (*often*) The children are very active after meals.
7. (*seldom*) The food at that restaurant is good.
8. (*usually*) Are Mr. and Mrs. Harvey at home in the evening?
9. (*always*) Do you study your English lessons at night?
10. (*never*) Dorothy and I watch television during the afternoon.
11. (*ever*) Why doesn't that student write his lessons carefully?
12. (*rarely*) Mr. Wilson has time to see visitors in the morning.
13. (*usually*) Don't you keep your important papers in that drawer?
14. (*ever*) Have you listened to that radio program?
15. (*always*) The director is in his office between 2:00 and 4:00 p.m.
16. (*usually*) Is there someone here before 9:30 a.m.?
17. (*never*) We have been to the Museum of Modern Art.
18. (*always*) Why do you study your lessons with Richard and Fred?
19. (*ever*) Does the foreman eat lunch with the other workers?
20. (*usually*) Are your English assignments difficult?
21. (*seldom*) That store receives complaints from its customers.
22. (*always*) Does that fellow do his share of the work?
23. (*often*) Mr. Johnson dictates reports to his secretary.
24. (*never*) That store closes before 5:30 or 6:00 p.m.
25. (*usually*) Are you ready for breakfast by eight o'clock?
26. (*ever*) Why don't you speak English with your friends?
27. (*often*) Mr. Hanson rides to work with Mr. Anderson.
28. (*always*) My former secretary did her work very promptly.
29. (*seldom*) Miss Stewart is sick or absent from work.
30. (*never*) Mr. Fox smokes cigars in the office during the day.
31. (*usually*) We learn many new words in our English class.
32. (*always*) They have tried to follow his instructions very carefully.

HEARING AND SPEAKING LESSON

Listen carefully. Answer the questions with a full sentence.

1 *That man is always late.*
2
3
4
5
6
7
8 *Are Mr. and Mrs. Harvey usually at home in the evening?*
9
10
11
12
13
14
15
16
17
18
19
20
21
22
23
24
25
26
27
28
29
30
31
32

WORD ORDER : REVIEW

Copy each sentence and add the indicated word or words in the correct position. Do not add any other words.

1. (*too*) Mr. Johnson bought a leather briefcase.
2. (*still*) Are you studying English at the same school?
3. (*usually*) We use that word in a little different way.
4. (*ever*) Have they visited that national park?
5. (*yet*) Are you accustomed to our climate?
6. (*also*) Our friends enjoy popular music.
7. (*to her*) William mailed the letter several days ago.
8. (*always*) Richard does his work at the last minute.
9. (*either*) The police didn't notice anything unusual.
10. (*still*) We don't have enough money to buy a new car.
11. (*him*) We sent a very practical gift for his birthday.
12. (*never*) They have visited the Scandinavian countries.
13. (*always*) Is your teacher strict about your homework?
14. (*yet*) Has the carpenter repaired the hole in the roof?
15. (*to us*) Our friends returned the photographs yesterday.
16. (*already*) Miss Peters has sent the letter, hasn't she?
17. (*always*) My secretary does her work very promptly.
18. (*still*) Do you find the English language simple?
19. (*either*) We didn't go to the meeting last Friday night.
20. (*to us*) Our teacher didn't explain the last assignment.
21. (*usually*) Does that new employee do his part of the work?
22. (*yet*) They haven't found a solution to that problem.
23. (*seldom*) Don and I go to that section of the city.
24. (*either*) Mr. Smith didn't finish his work, did he?
25. (*still*) There are plenty of sandwiches on the table.
26. (*always*) Have you been interested in that subject?
27. (*already*) You've done those two lessons, haven't you?
28. (*to them*) Has Miss Stewart sent that letter or not?
29. (*too*) There are many students in the second section.
30. (*still*) The foreman hasn't spoken to Mr. Johnson about it.
31. (*often*) Fred's brother stays with him over the weekend.
32. (*always*) Is there a guard in this building during the night?

HEARING AND SPEAKING LESSON

Listen carefully. Answer the questions with a full sentence.

1. *Mr. Johnson bought a leather briefcase too.*
2. *Are you still studying English at the same school?*
3.
4.
5.
6.
7.
8.
9.
10.
11.
12.
13.
14.
15.
16.
17.
18.
19.
20.
21.
22.
23.
24.
25.
26.
27.
28.
29.
30.
31.
32.

WORD ORDER : "PLACE," "MANNER," AND "TIME" 124

Put the expressions within the parentheses into the correct order. Then put these expressions at the end of the sentence. Do not add or omit any words. Study the examples carefully. In connection with the second group, remember "duration" and "accompaniment" take the same position as "manner."

"PLACE" AND "TIME"

1. They're studying their lessons (*right now - at the library*).
   —*They're studying their lessons at the library right now.*
2. Frank met Mr. Wilson (*on Thursday - at Mr. Hart's house*).
3. The boys ran (*down the street - a few minutes ago*).
4. The students studied the lesson (*yesterday - on page 80*).
5. Our friends flew (*to South America - last summer*).
6. I had a very bad cold (*two days ago - in my head*).
7. Roger and Frank went (*to a concert - on Wednesday night*).
8. That fellow studies with me (*every afternoon - at the library*).

"PLACE" AND "MANNER"

1. That student always comes (*on time - to this class*).
   —*That student always comes to this class on time.*
2. Did Tom and you go (*with your friends - to the movies*)?
3. The angry customer looked (*doubtfully - at the clerk*).
4. We are going to work (*at the library - for three hours*).
5. Elizabeth usually walks (*with her brother - to school*).
6. My friend and I ran (*toward the train - with our baggage*).
7. That employee seldom gets (*to the office - late*).
8. The secretary wrote the message (*on the paper - hastily*).

"MANNER" AND "TIME"

1. The students are pronouncing the words (*now - carefully*).
   —*The students are pronouncing the words carefully now.*
2. The students know the irregular verbs (*now - very well*).
3. Richard studies his lessons (*every night - for two hours*).
4. Our friends will arrive here (*quite early - in the morning*).
5. Mr. Brown did all of the work (*alone - last Thursday*).
6. Everyone criticized the man (*after the meeting - severely*).
7. Miss Foster described her vacation trip (*in detail - last night*).
8. Frank and I watched television (*last Saturday night - with Fred*).

HEARING AND SPEAKING LESSON

Listen carefully. Answer the questions with a full sentence.

"PLACE" AND "TIME"

1. They're studying their lessons at the library right now.
2. Frank met Mr. Wilson at Mr. Hart's house on Thursday.
3.
4.
5.
6.
7.
8.

"PLACE" AND "MANNER"

1.
2. That student always comes to this class on time.
3. Did Tom and you go to the movies with your friends?
4.
5.
6.
7.
8.

"MANNER" AND "TIME"

1.
2. The students are pronouncing the word carefully now.
3. The students know the irregular verbs very well now.
4.
5.
6.
7.
8.

WORD ORDER : DIRECT OBJECTS   125

Put the expressions within the parentheses into the correct order. Then put these expressions at the end of the sentence. Do not add or omit any words. Study the example carefully and review Exercise 124. Remember the direct object always follows the verb in English.

1. The Students know (*very well - now - the irregular verbs*).
   —*The students know the irregular verbs very well now.*
2. Elizabeth studies (*every evening - at home - her lessons*).
3. I pick up (*at the office - my paycheck - every Friday*).
4. Mrs. Brown chose (*without any difficulty - a dress - yesterday*).
5. Someone took (*last night - from my desk - my dictionary*).
6. I drank (*too much coffee - this morning - at breakfast*).
7. Their friend ate (*after the meeting - with them - lunch*).
8. Mr. Wilson bought (*an expensive camera - two days ago - there*).
9. Our team won (*last year - the championship - in this region*).
10. Cuba exports (*to the United States - much sugar - every year*).
11. We enjoyed (*very much - on Saturday night - Mr. Moore's lecture*).
12. You seldom hear (*on the radio - good programs - at this hour*).
13. We have studied (*up to now - carefully - every lesson*).
14. Mr. Smith borrowed (*two years ago - from a friend - the money*).

WORD ORDER : DIRECT AND INDIRECT OBJECTS   126

Follow the instructions given in Exercise 125. Also review Exercises 124 and 125.

1. My secretary sent (*last week - to them - the letter*).
   —*My secretary sent the letter to them last week.*
2. Miss Foster has described (*several times - her trip - to me*).
3. Mr. Hilton often brings (*after work - flowers - his wife*).
4. The teacher explains (*in class - to the students - the lessons*).
5. The Taylors sent (*a bracelet - their daughter - for her birthday*).
6. That girl showed (*Mr. Moore - after class - her homework*).
7. Mr. Smith sold (*to my friend - his old car - last week*).
8. Would you please lend (*for a few minutes - your pencil - John*)?
9. Their uncle built (*a year ago - a new house - for them*).
10. The customer gave (*reluctantly - the clerk - the money*).
11. Mrs. Johnson read (*a story - just before bedtime - her son*).
12. Fred showed (*to all of his friends - proudly - the photographs*).
13. Betty's mother made (*a lovely dress - her - for the party*).
14. The messenger handed (*the two boxes - carefully - to Albert*).

HEARING AND SPEAKING LESSON 125

Listen carefully. Answer the questions with a full sentence.

1. *The students know the irregular verbs very well now.*
2. *Elizabeth studies her lesson at home every evening.*
3.
4.
5.
6.
7.
8.
9.
10.
11.
12.
13.
14.

HEARING AND SPEAKING LESSON 126

Listen carefully. Answer the questions with a full sentence.

1. *My secretary sent the letter to them last week.*
2. *Miss Foster has described her trip to me several times.*
3.
4.
5.
6.
7.
8.
9.
10.
11.
12.
13.
14.

CONGRATULATION! YOU'VE GOT A DIPLOMA!
(PUT YOUR NAME ON YOUR DIPLOMA)

Certificate of Graduation

CERTIFICATE OF GRADUATION

FROM

New York Grammar School
NEW YORK GRAMMAR SCHOOL

Know All Men by These Presents
Know All Men by These Presents

that the Board od trustees by virtue of the authority vested in it by the
that the Board of trustees by virtue of the authority vested in it by the

Commission on Higher Education has conferred upon
Commission on Higher Education has conferred upon

YOUR NAME HERE

who has satisfactorily completed the prescribed course, the degree of
who has satisfactorily completed the prescribed course, the degree of

Graduation of Elementary & Intermediate American English Grammar
Graduation of Elementary & Intermediate American English Grammar

with all the rights, honors and privileges
with all the rights, honors and privileges

as well as the obligations and responsiblities thereunto appertaining,
as well as the obligations and responsiblities thereunto appertaining.

Give this _____ th day of _____ in the year of _____ .

_____
Head Teacher

_____   _____
Publisher   Asst. Teacher

LET'S GO TO THE ADVANCED & EXPERT COURSE!

APPENDIX

COMMONLY USED CONTRACTIONS

I am	*I'm*	*I will	*I'll*
you are	*you're*	*you will	*you'll*
he is	*he's*	will not	*won't*
she is	*she's*	*I would	*I'd*
it is	*it's*	*you would	*you'd*
that is	*that's*	would not	*wouldn't*
there is	*there's*	should not	*shouldn't*
who is	*who's*	can not	*can't*
what is	*what's*	could not	*couldn't*
we are	*we're*	must not	*mustn't*
you are	*you're*	*I have (gone)	*I've (gone)*
they are	*they're*	*you have (gone)	*you've (gone)*
is not	*isn't*	*he has (gone)	*he's (gone)*
are not	*aren't*	*she has (gone)	*she's (gone)*
was not	*wasn't*	*it has gone	*it's (gone)*
were not	*weren't*	have not (gone)	*haven't (gone)*
do not	*don't*	*I had (gone)	*I'd (gone)*
does not	*doesn't*	*you had (gone)	*you'd (gone)*
did not	*didn't*	had not (gone)	*hadn't (gone)*

GENERAL NOTE : The contractions with asterisks are not normally used in negative sentences with not. For example, in the sentence *he will not go*, the usual contraction is *he won't go*.

COMMONLY USED GRAMMATIC CONTRACTIONS

adj.	*adjective*	*Mr.	*a man's title*
adv.	*adverb*	*Mrs.	*a married woman's title*
anon.	*anonymous*	n.	*noun*
cf.	*compare*	par.	*paragraph*
conj.	*conjunction*	pl.	*plural*
e.g.	*for example*	prep.	*preposition*
et al.	*and others*	pron.	*pronoun*
ect.	*et cetra, and so forth*		

GENERAL NOTE : Contrary to the custom of many other countries, it is ordinary impolite or improper to address a man as *Mr.* or a woman as *Mrs.* without adding his or her family name. Incorrect an impolite : *May I ask you a question, Mr?* Correct and polite : *May I ask you a question Mr. Taylor?* In the United States, the word *Sir* is a correct and very polite title of address for a man either older or higher in position than speaker. For example : *May I ask a question Sir?*

COMMONLY USED IRREGULAR VERBS

	1ST FORM (Present)	2ND FORM (Past)	3RD FORM (Past Participle)		1ST FORM (Present)	2ND FORM (Past)	3RD FORM (Past Participle)
1	am	was	been	38	forgive	forgave	forgiven
2	are	were	been	39	freeze	froze	frozen
3	is[1]	was	been	40	get	got	got(ten)[2]
4	beat	beat	beat	41	give	gave	given
5	become	became	become	42	go	went	gone
6	begin	began	begun	43	grind	ground	ground
7	bend	bent	bent	44	grow	grew	grown
8	bet	bet	bet	45	hang	hung	hung
9	bite	bit	bitten	46	have	had	had
10	bleed	bled	bled	47	hear	heard	heard
11	blow	blew	blown	48	hide	hid	hidden
12	break	broke	broken	49	hit	hit	hit
13	breed	bred	bred	50	hold	held	held
14	bring	brought	brought	51	hurt	hurt	hurt
15	build	built	built	52	keep	kept	kept
16	buy	bought	bought	53	know	knew	known
17	catch	caught	caught	54	lay	laid	laid
18	choose	chose	chosen	55	lead	led	led
19	come	came	come	56	leave	left	left
20	cost	cost	cost	57	lend	lent	lent
21	creep	crept	crept	58	let	let	let
22	cut	cut	cut	59	lose	lost	lost
23	do	did	done	60	lie	lay	lain
24	dig	dug	dug	61	make	made	made
25	draw	drew	drawn	62	mean	meant	meant
26	drink	drank	drunk	63	meet	met	met
27	drive	drove	driven	64	pay	paid	paid
28	eat	ate	eaten	65	put	put	put
29	fall	fell	fallen	66	quit	quit	quit
30	feed	fed	fed	67	read	read	read
31	feel	felt	felt	68	ride	rode	ridden
32	fight	fought	fought	69	ring	rang	rung
33	find	found	found	70	rise	rose	risen
34	fit	fit(ted)	fit(ted)	71	say	said	said
35	flee	fled	fled	72	see	saw	seen
36	fly	flew	flown	73	seek	sought	sought
37	forget	forgot	forgot(ten)	74	sell	sold	sold

COMMONLY USED IRREGULAR VERBS

	1ST FORM (Present)	2ND FORM (Past)	3RD FORM (Past Participle)		1ST FORM (Present)	2ND FORM (Past)	3RD FORM (Past Participle)
75	send	sent	sent	94	strike	struck	struck
76	set	set	set	95	swear	swore	sworn
77	shake	shook	shaken	96	sweep	swept	swept
78	shoot	shot	shot	97	swim	swam	swum
79	shut	shut	shut	98	swing	swung	swung
80	sing	sang	sung	99	take	took	taken
81	sink	sank	sunk	100	teach	taught	taught
82	sit	sat	sat	101	tear	tore	torn
83	sleep	slept	slept	102	tell	told	told
84	slide	slid	slid	103	think	thought	thought
85	speak	spoke	spoken	104	throw	threw	thrown
86	spend	spent	spent	105	understand	understood	understood
87	spin	spun	spun	106	wake up	woke up	woken up
88	spilt	spilt	spilt	107	wear	wore	worn
89	spread	spread	spread	108	weave	wove	woven
90	spring	sprang	sprung	109	weep	wept	wept
91	stand	stood	stood	110	win	won	won
92	steal	stole	stolen	111	wind	wound	wound
93	stick	stuck	stuck	112	wring	wrung	wrung

GENERAL NOTE : The meaning of an irregular verb is sometimes changed by prefixing another word. This does not affect the form of the verb itself. Example : *undergo, underwent, undergone*. Other verbs of this type are *mislay, mislead, overhear, oversleep, overtake, overthrow, undertake, underwrite, undo, withstand*. A notable exception is the verb *welcome* which is regular in its forms *welcome, welcomed, welcomed*.
NOTE 1 : The infinitive of this verb is (to) *be*. This is the only verb in English which does not take the same form for the infinitive and the first person singular of the simple present tense.
NOTE 2: Since usage varies greatly on the choice of *got* or *gotten*, non-native speakers are usually confused and uncertain in using this verb. Much difficulty can be avoided by advising students to use only *got* for the present participle. Although ifi some cases this may conflict with local usage, the student will never be incorrect.

PERSONAL PRONOUNS AND ADJECTIVES

SINGULAR	SUBJECT PRONOUNS	OBJECT PRONOUNS	POSSESSIVE PRONOUNS	POSSESSIVE ADJECTIVES	REFLEXIVE PRONOUNS
1ST PERSON	I	me	mine	my book	myself
2ND PERSON	you	you	yours	your book	yourself
3RD PERSON	he	him	his	his book	himself
	she	her	hers	her book	herself
	it	it		its eye	itself
PLURAL					
1ST PERSON	we	us	ours	our book	ourselves
2ND PERSON	you	you	yours	your book	yourselves
3RD PERSON	they	them	theirs	their book	themselves

IRREGULAR COMPARATIVE AND SUPERLATIVE FORMS

POSITIVE DEGREE	COMPARATIVE	SUPERLATIVE	POSITIVE DEGREE	COMPARATIVE	SUPERLATIVE
bad	worse	the worst	little	less	the least
far	further	the furthest	many	more	the most
good(well)	better	the best	much	more	the most

THE VERB (TO) BE

TENSE	
GENERAL	be
PRESENT	I am (we are)
	you are (you are)
	he is (they are)
PAST	I was^1 (we were)
	you were (you were)
	he was^2 (they were)
FUTURE	I will be
PAST FUTURE	I would be
PERFECT PRESENT	I have been
PERFECT PAST	I had been
PERFECT FUTURE	I will have been
PERFECT PAST FUTURE	I would have been

THE PRINCIPAL PARTS OF THE VERBS

	1ST FORM	2ND FORM	3RD FORM
REGULAR	work	worked	worked
ILLREGULAR	give	gave	given

THE INFINITIVE

	ACTIVE	PASSIVE
PRESENT	work	worked
PERFECT	give	given

THE "ING" FORM

	ACTIVE	PASSIVE
PRESENT	giving	being given
PERFECT	having given	having been given

THE VERB (TO) GIVE

TENSE	ACTIVE		PASSIVE	
	SIMPLE - CONTINUOUS		SIMPLE - CONTINUOUS	
GENERAL	give - be giving		be given	
PRESENT	I give - I am giving[2]		I am given[2] - I am being given[2]	
	(he gives)[1]			
PAST	I gave - I was giving		I was given - I was being given	
FUTURE	I will give - I will be giving		I will be given	
PAST FUTURE	I would give - I would be giving		I would be given	
PERFECT PRESENT	I have given - I have been giving		I have been given	
	(he has given)[2] - (he has been giving)[2]		(he has been given)[2]	
PERFECT PAST	I had given - I had been giving		I had been given	
PERFECT FUTURE	I will have given		I will have been given	
PERFECT PAST FUTURE	I would have given		I would have been given	

GENERAL NOTE : Unless otherwise indicated, all persons(*I, you, he, she, it we they*) take the same form. For the third person singular, only *he* is given; however, this indicates that *she* and *it* take the same form. NOTE 1: The parentheses indicate that the third person singular(*he, she, it*) takes a different form from the form for the other persons. NOTE 2: The verb *be* is the auxiliary for the present and past tense in these columns. The verb *be* takes its form according to the paradigm given on the opposite page. Note that the principal part of the verb(*giving; given; being given*) does not change. NOTE 3: *I were* and *he were* after the verb *wish* and in unreal present conditional clauses after *if.*

U.S. MONETARY UNITS

BILLS(PAPER MONEY)		COINS(SILVER MONEY)	
$50.00 or $50	*fifty dollars*	$ .50 or 50¢	*fifty cents*
			a half dollar
$20.00 or $20	*twenty dollars*	$ .25 or 25¢	*twenty-five cents*
			a quarter
$10.00 or $10	*then dollars*	$ .10 or 10¢	*ten cents*
			a dime
$ 5.00 or $5	*five dollars*	$ .05 or 5¢	*five cents*
			a nickel
$ 1.00 or $1	*one dollar*	$ .01 or 1¢	*one cent*
			a penny
$ 1.25	*one dollar and twenty five cents or a dollar and a quarter.*		
$ 2.50	*two dollars and fifty cents or two and a half dollars or two fifty.*		
$128.50	*one hundred and twenty-eight dollars and fifty cents.*		
	one twenty-eight fifty.		

영어는 기본, 제2외국어는 경쟁력!

딱! 하루 만에 끝내는 일본어 첫걸음

BEST 3
일본어 첫걸음
장기 베스트셀러
2011~2013

릿쿄 랭기지랩 인스티튜트 | 지음
정가 | 12,000원

선택, 집중, 반복 전략으로 최단시간에 일본어 정복!

선택 : 자주 쓰는 문법만 골라서!
집중 : 짧은 시간에 몰아서!
반복 : 외워질 때까지 무한반복한다!

제2외국어로 경쟁우위를 점하라!

매일 쓰는 단어만 하루에 딱 10개씩!

BEST 5
일본어 어휘
장기 베스트셀러
2011~2013

릿쿄 랭기지랩 인스티튜트 | 지음
정가 | 13,500원

일상에서 자주 쓰는 단어만 골라 부담 없이 어휘력 확장!

실용 : 일본인이 실제로 쓰는 살아있는 단어만!
재미 : 외우다 질리지 않게 딱 10개씩!
상식 : 생생한 일본 현지 사정과 함께 배운다!